JOHN LOPER

SUPPORT

THE GOVERNMENT

YOURSELF

OTHERS

How To Succeed
In Government
Contractor
Employment

JOHN LOPER

SUPPORT

THE GOVERNMENT

YOURSELF

OTHERS

For permissions and inquiries, contact:
www.thejohnloper.com

First edition, 2025
Printed in the United States of America

ISBN: 979-8-99948120-7

Library of Congress Control Number: 2025914510

Book design by Matthew Clark
Cover Images:
Top View Of The United States Of America Flag On White Surface
By Lightfieldstudios
The dome of the United States capitol with an American flag isolated on white background
by DanThornberg
Edited by Jennifer Wallace

This book is a work of nonfiction. Some names and identifying details may have been changed to protect privacy.

John Loper
www.thejohnloper.com

Table *of* Contents

Part Two

"Knowing is not enough; we must apply. Willing is not enough; we must do."

Johann Wolfgang Von Goethe 51

INTRODUCTION

My hands were tied. We had to let the employee go.

Though I wasn't the prime lead, I felt responsible.

The reasons for the employee's termination: bad communication, bad integration, poor assumptions on my part (expecting everyone to understand the job), and failing to pass my knowledge, history, stories, and ideas on to my team leads. The employee wasn't doing a good job. The employee didn't communicate with the customer being supported, and didn't listen when the government said to work faster, respond faster, and communicate better. The employee didn't take it seriously when the government voiced other concerns. However, my team lead also didn't communicate—the lead never asked "How is work going? Do you need anything? Can I help you in any way?"

This was a learning experience for the team lead, who needed to provide more communication and support, and it was a learning experience for me. I should have set expectations and communicated them clearly. It was a huge letdown for the employee—I believe, if the communication had gone differently, the employee could have been placed on an improvement plan and, ultimately, redeemed themselves. Instead, because of how government prime and sub contracts work, I was out of the loop, and my hands were tied.

It was too late.

Some experiences in life bother you... They stick in your mind like a bad tattoo from your 20s. This is one of those experiences for me. In writing this book, I hope to create something positive for other people—I want good to come out of the moment when a person lost their job.

The employee started in August 2023, and at first, I only heard good reports. The employee was in the office when they were needed and learned the job well, including how to navigate the systems required for the position. I was in contact with the employee and site lead a few times within the first six months. The employee needed to work from various locations because they were taking care of family members. In the telework environment, such requests are normal, and the employee and site lead both said the government lead was aware of the need and on board with it. I thought nothing of it.

It all changed by February 2024, when I got an email from the prime contractor saying the government wanted to remove the employee for not completing the contracted tasks the employee was hired to do. This came as a huge shock to me. I made a few phone calls to figure out what was happening, and that's when I learned the government had been talking with the prime team lead about their concerns: slow response times and deliverables that required multiple reworks. These concerns never made their way to the site lead or me. I never got a direct answer from the prime about whether the site lead was told about the issues or if the site lead tried to take care of it on their own. I also learned the prime got an email two weeks before the employee was let go, requesting a plan of action for the employee to improve the quality of their support, but the email went unanswered. This was a major oversight for the prime lead and made it impossible for me to help repair the relationship between the support employee and the government.

During my investigation, I learned all the concerns the government brought up were valid, and because the government came to believe we'd been non-responsive about fixing the issue, I wasn't able to put the employee on a performance improvement plan or pull them into a guidance session.

Letting an employee go due to bad communication and failure to tackle the issues drove me to complete this two-part book. Over six million people provide direct support to the federal government, and of that number, over four million are contract employees. Over a million of those employees are within the first five years of their careers. Part one of this book is for government support staff in the first five years of their careers. Part two is for those who plan to advance to leadership in government support, as well as those who are thinking about it and want to strengthen their skills. My goal? To help millions of people secure government positions, grow stronger, and lead the future.

I believe you learn more from failing than you do from succeeding. When everything goes perfectly, you rarely stop and think about what drove the success.

It took time for me to grow into a person who can deal with different types of people, political motivations, and other characteristics that influence how they think and see the world daily. Now I have learned how to be adaptable, and I want to help you nurture the same attitude and character that's enabled me to be successful. A bit about me: I've worked with the federal government for nearly 20 years, both as an employee and a contractor supporting federal employees. I started as an intern, became an entry-level analyst, and skipped ahead to become a senior analyst. Eventually, I became a subject matter expert and program manager.

I've seen people in different roles—some people failed, and others thrived. I've seen contract support employees who couldn't handle not being the decision-maker, government employees who couldn't handle how slowly their managers made decisions, and employees who took it all in stride and navigated the support world to control their careers.

I've helped many people get their first job in the government, and I've helped over a dozen staff members secure their first leadership roles. This book is meant to help two types of people: those who want to work in the government and those who want to become leaders within the government world.

A key piece of advice (no matter what stage you're in) is to balance patience with action. Nothing in the government happens fast enough, but few in the government are aggressive enough, either. To succeed, learn when to wait and when to take action.

This is not a career for everyone, but it's a career anyone can have if they remove the barriers of entry and choose a job within the government that best suits their current field and personal skills. Did you know nearly any job available in the world—from mechanic to plumber to rocket scientist to pilot—is also available in the contractor realm of government support? Generally speaking, positions within government support provide a higher pay scale than those outside of government support.

This book won't work if you don't. Remember, the most important part of this journey is you and your willingness to engage. The opportunities are there for the taking. As you read, I encourage you to take notes so you can refer to them as you go. I hope this book also reminds you nothing is perfect—including jobs—and as long as you keep going, keep growing, and keep trying, you'll do great. The end depends on the beginning, so start with optimism.

I want you to be successful. Success isn't a straight line or elevator to the top. It looks different for everyone. Your definition of success is always changing. What you picture success as today is different from what you'll picture success as in five years. It's more like a winding road. Here are some examples of what I mean: I've succeeded at getting a government job just to quit, I got a team lead position just to quit, and I failed by not asking the right questions when I accepted a job. I didn't know what the job truly entailed. I've learned, gained more experience, reset my goals, and changed my definition of success. My successes were mixed with failure, which forced me to take a hard look at what was important to me and what I wanted to accomplish.

You don't have to take the path you see in movies, on TV, or in the lives of the people around you. You can live your life your way and change course as you see fit.

Strengths, Weaknesses, Opportunities and Threats

STRENGTHS	WEAKNESSES

OPPORTUNITIES	THREATS

At the beginning of each chapter, you will find a SWOT analysis sheet. This is an action item for you throughout this book. As you read each chapter, identify your strengths, weaknesses, opportunities and threats. These items are either going to help or hinder your future career. The goal is to help you see what you need to work on, what you are awesome at, what factors in life and work are in your favor, and what out there can potentially do you harm.

- **Strengths**: Strengths describe what you excel at and what separates you from others. Do you have a Master's degree? A certificate? Do you have specific skills or backgrounds aligning with the topic?
- **Weaknesses**: Weaknesses stop you from performing at top speed. These are areas where you need to improve to remain competitive. Are you not a people person? Does that matter in your career field? Are you not willing to geographically move?
- **Opportunities**: Opportunities are favorable external factors that could give you a competitive advantage. For example, being willing to fill difficult and stressful roles to grow and move up in a company.
- **Threats**: Threats refer to factors that can potentially harm you. For example, are new technologies coming out that can replace you? Is there anything you need to learn?

The key to remember in filling out the SWOT analysis is to be honest with yourself about your skills, and then use the information to create a plan to help your future. If you are not willing to be honest about who you are and what you are good and bad at, you will not get any value for your future out of the task.

This world is hard to break into, and once you are in, is competitive to grow in. The most successful people understand what they need to do and how to do it so they can get the best opportunities to grow into the future!

REMEMBER

It is vital to learn the rules and the craft before you can properly support the government, as government organizational structures and terminology can vary significantly.

If your career path is like mine, it can be unpredictable, but it's full of opportunity. This section guides you through the complex world of government support, where collaboration and understanding are key. I'll define roles and provide essential tools for effective engagement. The most critical insight? Success hinges on understanding your place within the realm of government support. Learn the "*what*" and "*why*" to become an indispensable part of this community. Dive in, and build the competence to succeed.

PART 1

SWOT ANALYSIS SHEET

STRENGTHS	WEAKNESSES

OPPORTUNITIES	THREATS

CHAPTER 1

Government Support Organizational Charts

"Success demands a high level of logistical and organizational competence."

— ATTRIBUTED TO GENERAL GEORGE S. PATTON JR.[1]

This chapter is not comprehensive, but it is meant to provide a general understanding of government support organizational charts. It would take many more books to provide a breakdown of specific areas of the government. Each department has different organizational structures and specific terms. Don't be surprised if you see different terms and titles than the example I provide. This is why it's vital to learn the rules and the craft before you can properly support the government.

The main takeaway from this section is many people work together to support the government. In addition to working with the government, you will work with the company that holds the contract with the government. (If you are working with a subcontractor, it adds yet another layer!) The organizational chart in the next few pages should give you an idea of what you'll deal with—skip ahead if you like visuals, then come back to this page.

Which PM is It—Program Manager, Product Manager, or Project Manager?

There are three similar titles in government support, and unfortunately, it can be confusing to determine which is which. Not every place defines these roles the same way… you'll probably find program managers who are doing project manager work and vice versa. Overall, though, the definitions below should be helpful in defining whose role is whose.

- **Program Manager:** Oversees, coordinates, plans, and executes multiple products and projects. Responsible for the overall cost, schedule, and performance success of items listed in the portfolio of the position. Within the government, this PM oversees contract status and contractor status. Ensures contractual/financial regulations and annual appropriations (and all other laws) are being followed. Executes requirements within the products and projects under their umbrella. Communicates with all parties, including other program managers in other offices, to ensure each program is serving the government at large.

- **Product Manager:** First-line management support for the program manager. The product manager executes each product under the direction of the program manager to ensure the end requirements of the project are met within cost, schedule, and performance requirements.

- **Project Manager:** First-line management support for the product manager. The project manager communicates day-to-day with internal government employees and external contractors who are directly executing the contracts to complete the specific project requirements, ensuring tasks are executed on time and on budget.

Each manager supports the one above by taking a smaller piece of the pie in order to offer support and meet government needs.

An Example of a Support Role Using an Organizational Chart

If you are getting started in government support as a logistics analyst, this is what your organizational chart could look like. You are the highlighted employee—the logistics analyst—working under a project manager who works under a product manager who works under a program manager who works for a larger command/organization/department. (Yes, even the names of the government divisions vary depending on which part of the government it is.)

As an entry-level logistics analyst, you'll support the logistics lead. However, you may (and probably will) support more than one project or program at a time. Why? Because not every project or program requires 40 hours a week of support, if you want to work full-time, you've got to supplement your income by working on a variety of projects and programs. (In case you're wondering, the average is about four to five projects or programs at a time. I've seen as low as one for a huge program and as high as 15 for smaller products.)

To put it simply, picture an organizational chart like the one above for every project or program you are working on… and then imagine trying to keep track of them all. It can become very confusing—not only do you have to keep the teams, protocol, and rules straight in your mind, but you have to focus on managing your time and each team's expectations regarding your availability. Remember, this is just for the side providing direct support to the government.

You also have to think about the company that gives you your paycheck (and maybe even the prime contractor over the company if you're a subcontractor). There is a different organizational chart for that side—and again, this is not what every organizational chart will look like, just a general idea of how the company structure could be set up. (If you are working for a subcontractor, everything to follow happens twice, since the prime contractor is over the subcontractor.)

Example of a Company Organizational Chart

This chart is simplified to make it easier to understand. In a more accurate chart, the VP of Program Management will have several program managers, and the program managers will have multiple task leads, and each of those will have multiple team leads under them.

In the government support organizational chart, you can see there's a chain of command, and there are multiple direct reports in the government. In the contractor world, you'll also have several people to report directly to.

Your requirements on the contractor side are as follows:

- Fill out your time card daily
- Complete and submit monthly status reports (the list of activities you are engaged in, activities completed, and activities coming up for the government)
- Submit travel request forms in the template and with supporting documents required by the contract
- Complete annual evaluations
- Complete annual HR needs
  - Benefit updates
  - Address changes
  - Life events
- Engage with security to ensure clearance is up to date and correct
- (Potentially) engage on a 6-month basis for your Common Access Card (CAC), which provides building and computer access for government support employees
- Submit leave requests
- Submit tuition reimbursement requests and finalizations
- And more

Proposals and Promotions

Companies are always trying to get more work, and in order to do that, they must bid on new contracts. Government requirements for proposals are written in a Request for Proposal (RFP). It's not unusual for a company to ask an employee to help write a proposal, since they're usually created based on current contracts, abilities, knowledge, and individuals within the company. By writing proposals when asked, you can gain more knowledge of (and provide more support to) the company you work with, enabling you to advance up the ranks.

Contractors aren't promoted on the government support side; they're promoted on the company support side. In order to be promoted, though, there has to be a position on a contract to promote you into. You have two options if you want to earn more money: grow on the company side while you look for a new position on a new contract with a new company, or wait for the current company to make the next level available to you (again, in this case, it would be the next level for a logistics analyst).

One More Thing

If you've learned anything from this chapter, it's that government support contractors can and will be pulled in many different directions. Remember Peter Gibbons from Office Space? He's not the only one with eight different bosses. [2]

REMEMBER

Government support roles involve navigating complex and often fluid organizational structures on both the government and contractor sides, requiring adaptability, effective time management, and the ability to manage expectations across multiple teams and reporting lines.

SWOT ANALYSIS SHEET

STRENGTHS	WEAKNESSES

OPPORTUNITIES	THREATS

CHAPTER 2

Get in the Door

"The will to win, the desire to succeed, the urge to reach your full potential… These are the keys that will unlock the door to personal excellence."

— CONFUCIUS (THE ANALECTS) [3]

Welcome to the beginning—it's time to strap on your boots and kick the door in. Getting started is often the biggest obstacle to success because of overwhelm. You may be fearful and worried about the daunting task ahead. This is natural—you have a long road ahead of you. However, whether you choose to walk the path of growth or the path of complacency, you are headed somewhere. Do you want to go somewhere you'll look back on with fond memories, or to a place of inaction that leaves you with regrets?

The path to government work has many barriers to entry, including education, experience, security clearance, job locations, travel requirements, and more. Certain barriers can be overcome depending on the uniqueness of the job you're chasing. For example, many FBI hackers may not pass security clearance and even have a record of committing cybercrimes. Because they have unique skills—skills the government needs—they are able to break down the barriers of entry. Obviously, I don't recommend this path, as it's a very risky and morally poor path to entry, but it's an example of one of the many paths leading to entering the workforce.

Here are (legal) ways to get a job in government support:

- **Join the military and retire after 20 years of service.** This path is both the easiest and the hardest. This affords you a great deal of knowledge, relationships, experience, education, and clearance, which opens nearly all barriers of entry for a government position. All that's left to do is to find an open position, interview, and get hired, but you'll start with a fantastic resume any government agency would find appealing. If you take this path, you will begin working for the government in your late 30s or early 40s.

- **Join the military and serve the minimum time.** Completing the minimum required time of service to get security clearance enables you to start looking for jobs as a government employee or contractor. This path is one of the most popular ones, but does come with risks, including deployments, calls back to service, and training injuries… all of which are also risks with the military career path above. However, compared to the first path, you will have limited knowledge, experience, relationships, and opportunities for education—these all help immensely with getting a position. It is possible, after four years in the service, to get an entry-level or internship position at the age of 22.

- **Apply for a government internship while still in high school.** These opportunities aren't available everywhere, but some government locations provide high school internships. An internship may offer some experience, clearance, and education, and can lead to long-term internships throughout your college years. This means you can be an intern from the ages of 16-22, graduate from college, and then jump into a mid-level position at 22 instead of an entry-level one.

- **Intern as a college post-graduate while pursuing higher education.** This was my path—I fell into the government support world. I had other goals, but they quickly fizzled out and lost their appeal. After high school and college, I became a government support intern at 24 years old by working on my MBA at night and interning full time with the US Army during the day. (My undergraduate degree qualified me for the internship.) I didn't have to make a ton of money because the internship paid for school and gave me experience in government. I did work side jobs to make extra money or to get free food and beer at restaurants. By 26, I had free beer (sometimes), a bachelor's degree, a master's degree, security clearance, government experience, and relationships enabling me to get the next full-time job post-internship and to graduate with an MBA.

These are just a few options… There are many more ways (like going to job fairs to talk to recruiters) to get in the door, and you can choose what works best for you. Some job boards online will show the requirements for government support jobs—create a plan to meet those requirements and attack.

Before you get started, know why you want to get in the door. (I'll ask you once more about whether you want to go into this line of work in chapter 15.) It might sound ridiculous, but knowing why you're doing the work will give you the drive to stay with it. Getting in the door can be challenging, lengthy, and disheartening. It's full of disappointments and false starts… but it is possible. If you're not sure why you're doing this, you'll have a harder time following through. Your "why" doesn't have to be lofty: it might be to make more money, live in interesting places, do something that matters, or follow your family's footsteps. It might change over time—in fact, I'd be shocked if it didn't change.

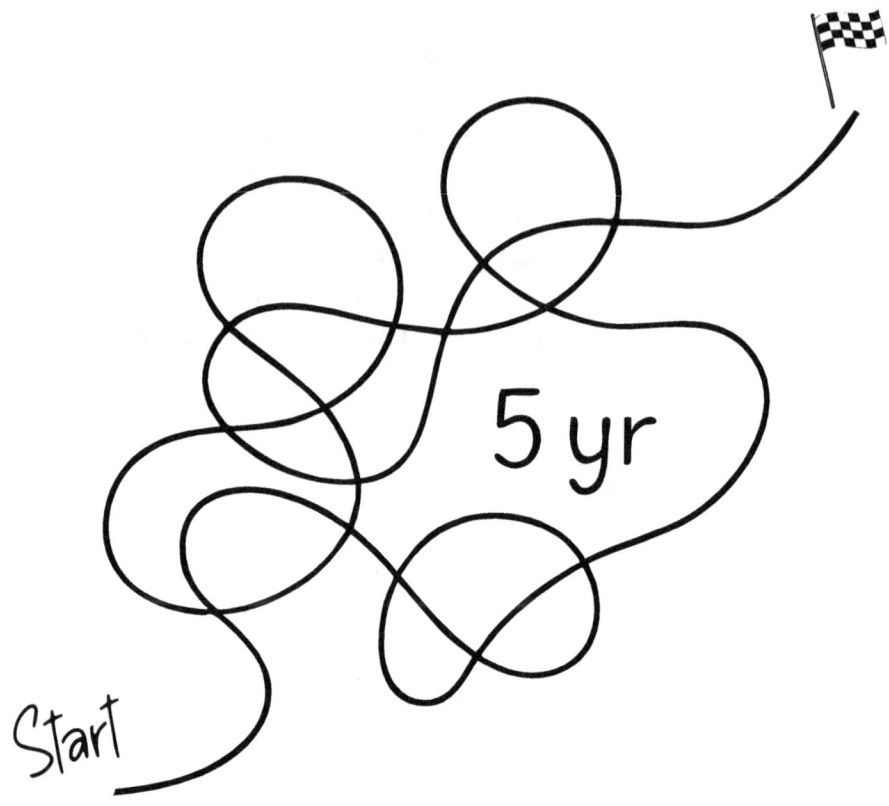

Most career paths aren't a straight line. For many of us, a career path looks more like this.

Look at the paths before you, and once you've chosen one, don't look back and ask "What if...?" The path you take will make you the person you'll become, and it's never too late to choose another path. Beat down the barriers, and don't stop because you got the job. Keep growing and looking for the next one.

Application Tips for Government Support Work

Relationship building is important in any line of work, but simply knowing someone won't be enough to get you an interview. You must be able to check all the boxes on your job description. Time requirements for relevant experience are real—if an application says it requires five years of experience using a specific software like GFEBS, which is the General Fund Enterprise Business System, you can't skate by with three years of experience. We don't always agree with the time or education requirements on the applications, but we must follow them. This process is called a "labor category validation," and it means the person hired for a position qualifies based on the description and requirements given.

If a company hires a person who doesn't qualify in the eyes of the government, and the government challenges the hire down the road, the company potentially has to pay back all the money invoiced to the government for the position. A preliminary search[4] found unqualified hires can cost as much as $4,000 just to hire a new employee, and small businesses could spend an additional $1,500 to train the new employee, not to mention the cost of lost productivity, since it takes between 42 and 50 days to fill a position in most companies. The company you're applying for has every reason not to hire you if you don't meet every requirement on the list. Don't waste your time or theirs.

What if a company doesn't attract qualified candidates? If this happens, the government could change the labor category for the job. I've seen labor categories for jobs that previously required a senior analyst changed so a journeyman can do it. I have never seen a company hire an under qualified person for a job—they will always ask the government to change the labor category rather than risk losing their contract and reputation with the government.

Once, an extremely "overqualified candidate" applied for a position, and their pay requirements were extremely high, over the contract rate. I asked the candidate about the real need for income, and then asked the government about adding a new labor category to the contract. My goal was to increase the rate of pay we could offer the overqualified candidate due to their level of experience, education, and time the candidate had in the field. This was also a challenging position to fill, which is why the government was willing to go through the pain of contract modification to add a new labor category.

Resume Tips

I always see recruiters or influencers telling people to have a one-page resume. This advice is garbage when it comes to government support.

In order, here are the most important items to include on your resume:

1. All the jobs you've worked
2. Your educational degrees
3. Required items for the job (double-check you've got them all)
4. Certifications you've obtained
5. Historic and current security clearances, as well as dates gained and last dates active
6. Detailed information for each part of your resume (where and when all the information on your resume occurred, and the impact your work had on you and those around you)

As an example of the kind of detail you're looking for, I have a line in my resume about when I was leading an over target baseline (OTB) review to show the government we completely understood contractor plans and budgeting. This saved the government $20 million by negotiating tasks, hours, and schedule considerations. You should show what you do and how it is impactful, list the company you were working for at the time, the government office you were supporting, and the dates of employment. Doing this builds trust and shows the validity of the work. Include the kitchen sink of employment history. My resume is seven pages long, with a ton of information about my experience, positions, education, requirements, and security clearance level. I make sure all the boxes are checked.

What not to include on your resume:
- Marital status
- Race

- Religion
- Date of birth
- Age (even if they can guess it based on your education)
- Other personal information protected by the law

Action Step

Track down your resume. Is it current? Does it check all the boxes listed above? If not, update it now. When you're done, continue reading this book.

Interview Tips

Some interview tips are good ("Arrive early"), and some are terrible ("Take control of the interview"). Before your interview, know what you're looking for and why. Make sure you also know how much money you really need versus how much you'd like to get. While you're in the interview, learn about the company you're applying for and the customer you're going to support. All of these factors go into whether you'll say yes to a job offer.

Don't go into an interview with generic, scripted questions from an AI bot. You shouldn't ask general questions—you should ask questions specific to you about the things that matter to you most. Is culture a priority to you? Then ask, "When was the last team outing, and what did you do?" If you want an opportunity for upward progress, ask, "Why did the previous employee leave the position I'm interviewing for?" Do you care about geographical mobility? Ask, "How many states or countries are your current employees in, and what type of work do they do?" Your questions are important: they allow both you and the company to see if you're a good fit. Asking your own questions is also a great way to get the interviewer to talk. People love to talk about themselves, so if you can get them to talk, they'll like you more. A leading question you could use is, "I see you did (this or that). What drove you to make that decision?"

Interviewing for a government contract job is different from interviewing for a government position or a "real-world job." The company you interview for could be in a position to say they like you and think you'll fit the position, or they might be a subcontractor to another company that holds the contract with the government, in which case, the process could take longer. The subcontracted company you interviewed with may require you to meet the prime contractor, and the prime contractor may require you to meet the government customer. These opportunities are important and are more about judging fit for you with the customer (government) than they are about your technical ability in the job, since the government is not allowed to tell the contractor whom to hire. However, every meet and greet is an opportunity for influence.

I don't care for multiple interview rounds. In some cases, you have to deal with them, but occasionally, you're in a position to interview with a prime who has a good relationship with the government and can say, "We like this person, they qualify, and they're getting an offer." If you'd like, though, you can also ask for a government meet and greet. I like to offer this even if the government doesn't request it because of the nature of government support: I might hire you as an employee of my company, but you'll be working on-site with the government, and you'll only see me a few times a year. The rest of the time, your relationship with the government is critical—they are the ones you'll see daily. Even a small meet and greet can help you get to know the people you'll be working with and decide if you want to work in that specific office.

One More Thing

Relax. Even if you don't get the job after an interview, the world will keep spinning and more opportunities will come your way... especially if you remember to keep growing and building relationships. For all you know, this specific job interview might turn into a call back from the same company six months later for a new position they just won. Engage, learn, grow, and always be ready for upcoming opportunities.

REMEMBER

Before you get started, know why you want to get in the door. ... knowing why you're doing the work will give you the drive to stay with it.

SWOT ANALYSIS SHEET

STRENGTHS	WEAKNESSES
OPPORTUNITIES	THREATS

CHAPTER 3

Learn the Rules

"The education of a man is never complete until he dies."

— ROBERT E. LEE (AS QUOTED IN PETER'S QUOTATIONS: IDEAS FOR OUR TIME BY LAURENCE J. PETER) [5]

Congratulations! You got the job, and now you're in government support. Now what? If you think you know everything and all you have to do is work and learn on the job, you're going to fail to provide solid support to the government. (Trust me—I've thought long and hard about how differently my first government job could have gone had I known better!)

Think of it this way: the best players in the NFL aren't content to just show up to games. They spend hours reviewing plays and taped games. They spend hours in the gym and on the practice field. They spend hours off-season working out unofficially with teammates and friends. They eat, sleep, and breathe football. What happens to the players who don't do that? What happens to the ones who party more than they practice, or think it's going to be easy because they were the best players in their old environments? They wake up and realize everyone on the field was the best player too, but some practiced more than they did, and this is a different world.

If you want to succeed in government, you have to start like many top NFL players do: by reading. You need to know the "play" for your particular line of work and everything encompassing it, whether you're in acquisition, engineering, logistics, contracts, etc. You don't know what you don't know, and you'll be surrounded by people telling you how to do your job. If you're not reading, it'll be a lot harder to tell whether you're getting bad advice or good advice.

Bad Advice

I've been told this many times: "I've been doing this for over 20 years, and this is how we do it." Don't trust people who tell you this. Most of the people who say this haven't read the rules the entire time they've been employed in government support, and chances are, they've been doing the job wrong for most of their employment.

Good Advice

The rules for government support are always changing, so one of the most important things to do is to keep up-to-date on what the rules are. You should review the rules at least once a year.

Keep in mind the rules are often written in an ambiguous way, and because of this, there can be a lot of confusion about how to apply them. It took me a long time to realize the government does this on purpose so broad regulations can be interpreted differently by each department, but writing rules ambiguously definitely has its pitfalls, like reading the same item multiple times and still not knowing exactly what it's trying to say.

One example of a rule that can be interpreted in two ways is the DoD 7000.14-R.[6] This regulation talks about the "colors" of government money, how different "colors" of government money can be used, and when they can be used. You might be thinking, "Money is green, and people can use it anytime." This is generally true in the US, but the government operates on a different level. Funds for government projects have expiration dates and are given specific colors based on the project phase. Funds allocated by the government must coincide only with their specific "color of money."

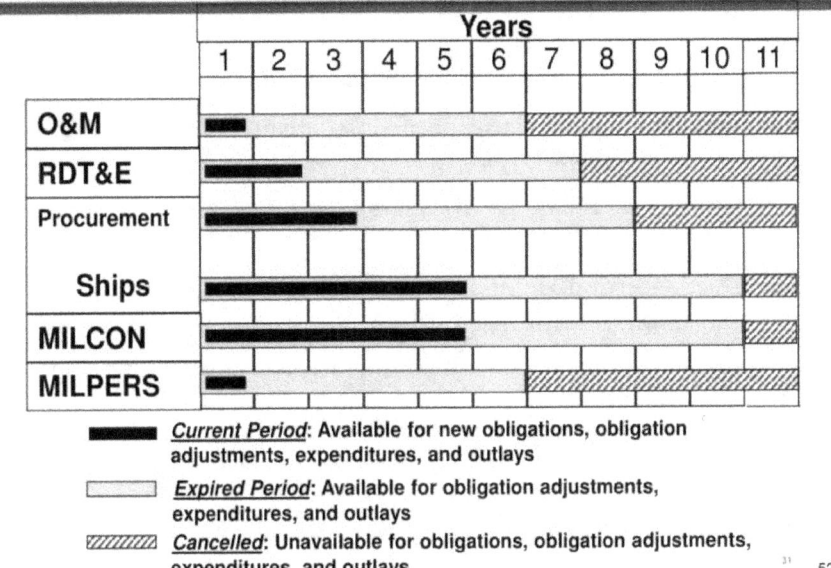

The *"colors of money"* shown above are O&M, RDT&E, Ships, MILCON, and MILPERS.

There are five main appropriation categories (or "colors of money") in the Department of Defense: Research, Development, Test and Evaluation (RDT&E); Procurement; Operation and Maintenance (O&M); Military Personnel (MILPERS); and Military Construction (MILCON).

Colors of Money in the Government

- **Research, Development, Test, and Evaluation (RDT&E):** [7] These fund contractor and government activity efforts needed for Research and Development (R&D) of equipment, material, and computer application software. This also funds Tests and Evaluations (T&E) to include Initial Operational Test and Evaluation (IOT&E)[8] and Live-Fire Test and Evaluation (LFT&E).[9] Finally, RDT&E funds

the operation of dedicated R&D installations activities for the conduct of R&D programs.
- Available for two years

- **Procurement:** These fund acquisition programs approved for production and all costs needed to deliver a useful end product.
  - Available for three years
  - Ships available for five years

- **Operation and Maintenance (O&M):** These fund civilian salaries, travel, minor construction projects, operating military forces, training and education, depot maintenance, stock funds, and base operations support.
  - Available for one year

- **Military Personnel (MILPERS):** These fund salary costs and other compensation for active and retired military personnel and reserve forces.
  - Available for one year

- **Military Construction (MILCON):** These fund major projects: bases, schools, missile storage facilities, maintenance facilities, medical/dental clinics, libraries, and military family housing.
  - Available for five years

Most projects require several colors of money before they're seen through to completion. Say you want to build a helicopter. You'll first apply for funds in the color of RDT&E (Research, Development, Testing, and Evaluation) so you'll know how the helicopter should be built. Once you have plans to build it, you'll move to the color of Procurement, then the color of O&M. Some people interpret the DoD 7000.14-R to mean all the funds have to be used up before the end of the current period, while others interpret it to mean all the funds have to be allocated to a contract before the end of the current period. These two interpretations have a major impact on how government money is spent, and conflicting interpretations can cause a lot of problems during a project. Operations and maintenance, for example, have a current period of just one year, so people who take a hardline approach to the regulation think they need to spend all the funds (completely use them up) within the first year. However, as you can see on the chart above, it's perfectly acceptable to continue using funds during the expired period (as long as those funds were put on a contract before the end of the current period).

If there's a disagreement about interpretation, the opposing parties should just go to those who wrote the regulation and ask, but that's not what usually happens. (I don't understand it—just communicate, people.)

When you run into a rule that can be interpreted two ways, find out which interpretation they follow at your workplace and use that interpretation. You can ask why it's interpreted that way if it doesn't make sense to you, and hopefully, you'll get a valid reason. If not, at least maybe someone will be willing to give it another look to ensure they're interpreting it correctly. However, even if the answer you get isn't satisfactory, the most important thing is to follow the interpretation everyone else is following, as failing to do this is what's most likely to be flagged during a government audit. During an audit, your workplace will have to provide the policies and processes it follows, including the interpretations of the rules. As long as everyone's following the same interpretation, the audit will generally be successful, and no one will get into trouble.

You've got to read up on the rules—but where do you look to find them? Thankfully, the government is good at providing generic training geared toward your career field (Contracts 101, Systems Engineering, Logistics 101, etc.). Each of these classes also talks about the laws and regulations driving the class. Most people gloss over them and try to click through as fast as possible to get to the real work, but wise employees treat them as the tools they are, digging down into the roots of the rules that created the training. As you're researching those rules created the training, you'll find they point to other documents and laws, and you'll eventually see a spider's web of why the government operates the way it does. These rules will become the foundation of your career and, though they are constantly changing, give you confidence you can carry with you anywhere.

One more note on learning the rules: aim not just to learn the rules of the job you're doing, but the rules of the entire contract you're working on. You may run across people who say, "That isn't my job," and if you're coming from a different environment, it can sound lazy. However, in the government support world, it's a very real problem, and there is a reason you're hearing it. If you cross the lines of your contract into other duties, you can get into trouble for it. I can't stress this enough: as contractors, we are paid to do what we're contracted to do—nothing more.

Sticking to your contractual duties may sound easy, but it can get tricky. Obviously, if your job is to track financials and you're asked to cut the grass, that's clearly beyond the contract, but if you're asked to review a statement of work or earned value data, the lines aren't as clear. This is why it's important to understand what requirements are within your purview and what items are not. If you're asked to do a task you shouldn't be doing, you've got to learn how to address it with the government. Again, this is not because you don't want to do the work, but because, as we will discuss later, your job is to keep the government out of trouble.

Still not sure about something? Talk with your task lead or project manager about your responsibilities. If you're not sure about a regulation, there are a few resources you can turn to. The main person to talk to would be the person making the decision about the interpretation (this could be a contracts person with a legal review, or someone in the program who's seen it before). If you want more general information about regulations, check out the DAU website or Acqnotes, which is basically Reddit for government contractors.

You'll need a whole lot of drive, patience, and determination to be great at your job. Patience is an ally and an enemy: without it, you won't gain perspective and will charge quickly into oblivion, but with too much of it, opportunities will pass you by because you won't act. Appreciate where you are now while making a plan to "eat the elephant one bite at a time."

How Am I Supposed to Remember All These Rules?

Think about how you learn best. Most people prefer a layered approach to learning, but also have a preferred learning style or two. What are yours?

Visual	Auditory
Visual learners prefer charts and graphs, lesson outlines, picture ads, and PowerPoint presentations.	Auditory learners enjoy listening to podcasts and audiobooks. They discuss or repeat what they've learned to others.
Reading/Writing	**Kinesthetic**
People who learn best by reading/writing prefer to use books and dictionaries to learn, and are proficient note-takers.	Kinesthetic learners take a hands-on approach to learning. They learn best when moving or interacting with the material.

Another approach is to try memory tricks. Here are some of the most tried-and-true methods:

- **Repetition.** Remember doing multiplication drills in school, day in and day out? There was a reason for it—repetition is consistently linked to memory. [10]

- **Understanding.** It's difficult to remember what you don't understand. If you're not sure, ask someone, and then, even better, explain it to someone else! [11]

- **Review (before sleep, if possible).** Take time before you sleep to review what you've learned that day. This transfers the information to your long-term memory. [12]

- **Use mnemonics.** In school, we learned the order of operations using "Please Excuse My Dear Aunt Sally." This is an example of mnemonics, another proven method [13] to learn.

- **Make a song for it.** Music is another secret weapon when it comes to learning and memory. [14] Try to find a song to help you remember. If there isn't one, use a favorite tune and make your own. Not naturally creative? You can still listen to lyric-free music to help concentrate.

REMEMBER

When you run into a rule that can be interpreted two ways, find out which interpretation they follow at your workplace and use that interpretation. ... the most important thing is to follow the interpretation everyone else is following, as failing to do this is what's most likely to be flagged during a government audit.

SWOT ANALYSIS SHEET

STRENGTHS	WEAKNESSES

OPPORTUNITIES	THREATS

CHAPTER 4

Learn the Craft

"You do not just wake up and become the butterfly—
growth is a process."

— RUPI KAUR, THE SUN AND HER FLOWERS [15]

How is learning the craft different from learning the rules? There are some key differences between the two, as the chart below shows. This chapter will go more in-depth about what learning the craft means, but if you're a visual learner, take a quick look.

The Rules	The Craft
Foundation of your career	House of your career (determines how big you build it, how you build it, how many floors you add)
Matter, but can be an obstacle (or are seen as an obstacle by other team members)	How you navigate the rules and the job
Some teammates are more interested in circumventing rules than following them, but this can actually increase the time a job takes	Ability to know & understand the rules, taking action to meet requirements as quickly as possible

As you can see above, if the rules are the foundation of your career, the craft is the house. It determines the size of your career and how you build it. Just as a foundation is useless if no one builds on it, knowing the rules is useless if you don't build on it by learning the craft or how to navigate the job itself. The main priority of leadership in the government is to get the job done, but sometimes the rules can be seen as obstacles to the goal. When a rule or requirement "gets in the way" of accomplishing a goal, it can be tempting to find a way around it… But often, this results in extra paperwork that could take longer than following the rule in the first place. Knowing the craft is knowing and understanding the rules, while communicating well and working in your team to accomplish the goals set before you as quickly as possible.

At the start of my career, a manager told me, "You are so right, but you are so wrong." I knew the rules and not the craft. I talked until I was blue in the face about regulations and how to get to the finish line, but I didn't understand how to make something of it. I didn't realize it wasn't just about following rules. It was also about supporting the government and getting the buy-in of the team and leadership on the way to the finish line. I was lucky to watch as this leader took what I said about regulations and turned it into a schedule with actionable steps. The leader got the buy-in from the team members who had to complete the steps in the schedule, and shared pain and celebrated successes along the way.

I didn't feel lucky in the moment, though. At the annual Christmas party, my manager got the "Employee of the Year" award. I got nothing. No "Rising Star" award, no big pat on the back. At the time, I thought, "Managers take all the glory. I deserved the award." I was passed up for an award I thought I had coming to me. It took years for me to understand that I didn't get it—I deserved to be sitting in my chair, mad, because there's a difference between knowing what you should do and succeeding at it. The manager deserved the award because he was able to take my skills and multiply them with his to create solid support in the government. I've been recognized for awards many times since, but even today, the lesson from not being recognized early on in my career has been the most meaningful to me.

Culture

Another important element of the craft is culture, and part of it is the specific government agency you're supporting. I have been able to support the Army, Navy, FBI, ATF (Department of Alcohol, Tobacco, Firearms, and Explosives), NASA, and the Missile Defense Agency. Each of these government entities has a different culture, but there are many similarities as well. One example of a difference between government work and traditional companies is how you'll address leadership. As a contractor, you'll be addressing employees of multiple ranks/statuses (everyone from entry-level interns to four-star generals), so it's vital to know how to do so. In some traditional companies, people address each other on a first-name basis. This is not a normal occurrence in government support, and wouldn't go over well at all.

However, there may be some similarities to traditional companies. In some companies, it's common to call people "Mr./Mrs., Sir/Ma'am," and based on the timing or place, it may be the expectation in government support as well. In the military, though, people are addressed by their rank in all communications (whether verbal or written).

In addition to how you address people, culture can make a difference in:
- Where you are in the chain of command
- How you talk
- How you dress
- How you take breaks

It's not easy to know what environment you're going into and what the expectations are, so before you accept a contracted position, ask.

Here are some questions to help you get a better picture of what the culture is like:

- What's the office like?
- Who are the people?
- How do they interact?
- What do they wear? (Ties, T-shirts, etc.?)
- Is it a "drinking buddy" kind of shop?

Remember, you get a vote on where you work. Sometimes getting a foot in the wrong door causes more harm than good. If you're not a "drinking buddy" type, are you going to enjoy an office where that's the environment? Knowing who you are and how far you're willing to bend to fit in will help you make the decision. Yes, going outside your comfort zone can help you grow, but going too far outside it may be the wrong choice for you.

Flexibility and Humility

Another part of learning the craft is being adaptable. Realize you don't know everything and probably never will. Careers evolve, and rules change. Knowing the craft is being a go-to person who can tell when it's time to ask someone for help. (It's also knowing whom to ask.) When you've learned "everything," keep learning the job, the rules, and the craft. Look around— the most successful people are always learning, always reading, and always growing. Review GAO (Government Accountability Office) rulings and federal procurement laws/guides/codes at least every quarter to stay on top of changes. Things are always changing; it is one of the hardest and simplest truths of life.

You'll Be Bored Sometimes

Believe it or not, learning the craft also includes being okay with boredom. Learning to accept boredom is especially important early in your career. You are paid to be available. You might feel like you're just sitting on your hands, or your talent is being wasted. I know how you feel—I've been there myself, and left some jobs for the same reason. I regret some of those decisions, and I realize others were the right decisions for me at the time.

Here are some activities you can do during downtime:

- Read
- Review the rules
- Meet new people
- Get more experience
- Find new tools for your work
- Talk to other employees/people in your field about what they're working on
- Learn what to do in your line of work and what not to do

Only you will know what your tipping point is between boredom and stagnation. It's important to feel like a strong, competent team member who can continue to grow in the future, but it's also important to be protected from the unknown in the job world. While you don't want to stay at a job where you're not being utilized, you may not find satisfaction by moving on. Sometimes the grass really is greener, but sometimes the green is just paint that washes away.

Deadline Communication Tips

One of the biggest parts of learning the craft is interacting with people in the right way. That's why I've devoted several chapters to communication. One of the things you'll constantly be working on is managing the deadlines placed against you. The government loves to track how long tasks take—in contracts, it's called the PALT (Procurement Administrative Lead Time). PALT tracks the time needed to complete the actions resulting in a contract being awarded. Timelines and deadlines are important in the government, driving decisions about the viability of a schedule, when to request funding, etc. Even at the beginning of your career, you'll be a key part of the decision-making process, since your ability to deliver has a direct effect on people who will be working on the project downstream.

A good rule of thumb when it comes to communicating about timelines is "Don't overpromise, but do everything you can to overdeliver." Be honest about the amount of time a task could take and explain why. Talk about the touchpoints and approval along the way, the potential reviews and re-works. Be honest about how long it will really take... but know, in many cases, your estimated timeline will be disregarded. Don't take it personally; that's just how it works in the world of government. Your job is to save the email communications and put them on record to show the baseline expectation is provided.

When you're given an unreasonable task, do it to the best of your ability. Don't skip steps or break rules to get it done faster, but do communicate where you're at with the task. You can (and should) communicate with leaders about how your tasks are progressing and what the next steps will be.

There are two reasons to communicate with leaders:
  a) Communication is a good practice in general
  b) The influence of leaders may be able to help get tasks done faster than usual

Again, don't overpromise, but definitely overcommunicate the status of the project.

REMEMBER

Knowing the rules is useless if you don't build on it by learning the craft or how to navigate the job itself.

SWOT ANALYSIS SHEET

STRENGTHS	WEAKNESSES

OPPORTUNITIES	THREATS

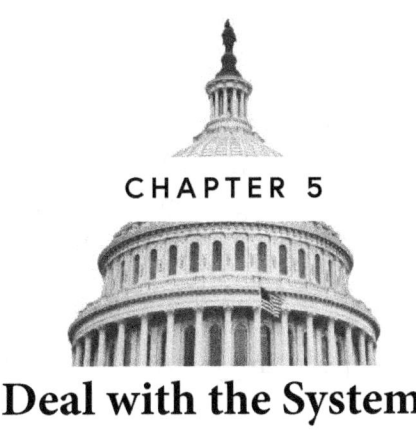

CHAPTER 5

Deal with the System

"...When you don't like a thing... change it.
If you can't change it, change the way you think about it."

— MAYA ANGELOU, WOULDN'T TAKE NOTHING FOR MY JOURNEY NOW [17]

The system is how the government ensures every "t" is crossed and every "i" is dotted. The best employees and companies can navigate the system while supporting the government. In some cases, it's how the government double-checks work, but in other cases, dealing with the system means being patient about inefficiencies or government workers' deficiencies.

Transitioning to government work as a high performer is not easy. I've worked with a lot of strong, knowledgeable people, and I've noticed they are often the ones who have the hardest time dealing with the system of the government. The biggest challenge for them is not what you would think... most high performers struggle because the system doesn't give them enough of a challenge.

Challenges of Dealing with the System

Here are some of the complaints I've heard from high performers who've made the move to government support:

- "I didn't get a response in a timely manner."
- "They changed just one word in my government review... not because it added value, but because they had the power to do it. Ridiculous!"

- "The review process takes too long."
- "I shouldn't have to provide documents to the government to prove I did my tasks. The government should just trust me!"
- "Why can't I just do my job? Why do I have to do annual training every year?"
- "Why do I need so much backup documentation for my travel requests? Why doesn't the government trust I'm following travel rules?"
- "Why do I have to fill out my timecard every day? I work for eight hours at a time, it doesn't change. Can't I just fill it out later?"
- "Why do I have to fill out my Monthly Status Report (MSR) at the end of every month? I do the same job every day."

I get it—I've had many of these complaints myself. Many government requirements for contract employees are time-consuming at best and downright annoying at worst.

The Other Perspective

However, I can also see where the government is coming from. The government has rules for a reason… and if people were perfectly following the rules and guidelines, there would be no need for them in the first place. The people saying "trust me" are often the ones who don't know what the rules are.

Here's an example: Did you know when you're renting a car for government contract work, you're supposed to choose the lowest-priced option available and decline additional insurance? Or, when you're booking a flight, you're supposed to choose non-refundable tickets? Most people don't know this when invoicing the government for travel reimbursement.

Regarding the complaint about MSRs, I'd say just because you're providing the same general support each month doesn't mean you're performing the same tasks. If you're an acquisition professional preparing a contracts requirement package, for example, the process takes several months from start to finish.

Here are some documents you might be working on during that time:
- Market research
- Independent government cost estimates
- Statement of work
- Contract deliverables
- And more

All of the above documents are created at different times and need to be documented on the MSR for the month in which they were made. Again, the government likes to track how long tasks take, and you do different tasks month to month, so they want you to document it with an MSR.

Here are a few more reasons why the government wants you to turn in an MSR every month:
- It's an automatic status report for the government and the company you work for
- It gives the government an idea of how long it takes to do tasks (which helps with creating time frames for future acquisitions)
- It gives the company insight into your work, which they can use to secure more proposals in the future
- It's important to many people downstream in the project

I do something to make MSRs as painless as possible, and maybe this will help you too:
1. On the first day of the month, I start an email draft and list all of the meetings I am going to do that month: integrated product team meetings, program tag-ups, financial reviews, and more
2. As I am given tasks and as I work on them, I add them to the draft, updating as I go
3. On the last day of the month, I open the email draft and copy and paste the notes to the MSR template for the contract, then send it off

Doing it this way has several benefits. The process is faster for you than racking your brain at the end of every month, trying to remember what you did. It's better for the government and the company than it would be if you were sending off generic bullet points, since you'll have a summary of each specific meeting and task you accomplished each month. Taking the time to list out sentences after a task is better than spending hours on it at the end of the month.

How to Complain Well

I know what you're thinking… "Really? Aren't you going to tell me about being a perfect employee, a team player, and a person who succeeds in life? Shouldn't you tell me not to complain?" I could, but complaining is normal. Everyone needs an outlet. Don't think you're the only one who gets frustrated from time to time. What's up to you is how you deal with frustration. The truth is, being successful includes knowing whom to complain to, how to complain, and when to complain.

Let's start with whom not to complain to. Never vent down. In other words, don't vent to people who report to you. Part of your job is to show competence and strength. Complaining to those who report to you undermines your leadership and their view of your ability to handle difficult situations. Likewise, don't vent sideways. Never complain to your peers. Why? Because if you get promoted after venting to a peer and they're not promoted, you have just vented down.

Whom to Vent To

If you can't vent down or sideways, then the correct way to vent must be up, right? Yes, but it can be tricky. You've got to let your frustration out, but you should never vent just for the sake of venting. Whenever you vent, you should have a purpose. Come up with two to three solutions that can potentially solve the problem you're venting about. Doing this will show you care about the company and want to improve things, and it'll show you don't expect everyone to fix it for you. (More about how and when to complain in chapter seven.)

You can also vent outside. No, not outside the company, but outside of your specific chain of command. This person should have a basic understanding of your sphere of interaction, but not be directly involved with it. This is a "sweet spot" when it comes to venting: they'll understand the challenges you face without being directly affected by them. As an example, if you were a program manager and you vented to the director of finance or the director of operations, this would be "venting outside."

What's the difference between venting up and venting outside? When you vent up, you are venting to someone. When you vent outside, you can vent with them. (They can vent to you and you can vent to them, which is not going to happen in a "venting up" situation.)

Venting outside comes with unique benefits and challenges. The benefits are both parties can gain valuable insight across company lines, see the company on a larger scale, and become more adept at spotting potential issues and fixing them before they become a bigger problem. That said, venting outside does come with risks, and you should always take time to get to know the other person and ensure they have your best interests at heart before you decide to vent to them. Choosing the wrong person can open you up to the office gossip pool and create a path where your personal feelings become public knowledge and undermine your advancement within the system. Choosing the right people for your circle takes time, and if you're smart, you'll share like a water faucet opened a little at first, and then share fully and openly after the trust is built.

Life Isn't Fair

Another part of dealing with the system is remembering life isn't fair and not everyone is treated equally. In a perfect world, we'd all get along great and go on never-ending vacations because we don't have to work anymore. Obviously, that's not the world we live in. Sometimes the system works in your favor and you have everything you need. People work well with you, and you smile when you wake up in the morning to go to work. Other times, you dread going to work, feel like an outsider, and struggle every day just to get answers.

I've been on both sides of the coin, and it may surprise you to hear I left both jobs. What I learned is you have to keep your eyes open for the next opportunity when you have a bad experience at the workplace, and even when you've got a great workplace, you will eventually have to move on to the next step. (Even the best experiences have to end sometime.) Learn to see your workplace experiences for what they are... ever-changing whirl-winds of happiness, frustration, opportunity, disappointment, and time you won't get back. If you use your time right, though, it'll help you in the future.

Dealing with Big-Picture Changes

People have an especially hard time dealing with the fact the big picture is always changing. They work on a project for years—decades, even—and then a new administration comes into the government and the program they spent years on gets canceled. They take it personally. Here are my two cents: a canceled program is not a reflection of your work, it is a reflection of the changing times. We don't still shoot bows and arrows in war—we have guns, drones, and space cameras. Times and technologies change. Realize it is changing faster than ever and be happy about the great accomplishments you achieved instead of being sad the program was canceled for the next big thing.

REMEMBER

The best employees and companies can navigate the system while supporting the government.

SWOT ANALYSIS SHEET

STRENGTHS	WEAKNESSES

OPPORTUNITIES	THREATS

CHAPTER 6

Home and Away

"The journey, not the arrival, matters."

— ATTRIBUTED TO T.S. ELIOT [18]

Government contractors were working remotely before remote work was a thing. Not every person who works within the sphere of government travels, but in many cases, you'll have to travel anytime from once or twice a year to once or twice a month. How much you travel depends on the position you have and the office you support.

Below are some examples of jobs I've worked and how much travel was required:

- Financial analyst — usually no travel required (maybe once a quarter at the most)
- Program integrator — 1-2 times a month
- Acquisition specialist — 1-2 times a quarter
- Test engineer - weeks at a time for long tests on site (up to 3 times a year)
- Program managers - don't bother buying a house... You won't be there

If you don't like to travel and can't see yourself in a financial analyst role, are there any options available to you? There may be, but you have to know what questions to ask first.

Here are some questions you can ask to know how much travel is required for a role you're considering:

The question	What it tells you
"Does the program have geographically diversified offices?"	If there are geographically diversified offices, chances are you'll need to travel to some of them.
"What products are we managing, and are those contractors providing support in the local area or in other locations?"	If contractors provide support in the local area, there will likely not be much travel required. However, if support is offered to other locations, you will probably need to travel.
"What does the office do?"	If the office you're working at builds things, you'll probably need to travel to different sites to perform inspections, tests, etc.
"Is all travel based in the US, or will I travel overseas as well?"	This will give you an idea of what extent to which you'll be traveling. I have worked overseas in Poland and Romania, as well as only within the US (with monthly trips to Washington, DC, or another state)

"Is there a chance the amount of travel I do will change? In what cases may that be possible?"	This will give you an idea of what could happen if anything changes within the contract. I had one job that started with travel once a year, but as the contractor overran the contract, I found myself traveling once a month to the office to track status, interview managers, etc.

You'll need to consider travel when deciding where you'll work. If you're working for a program office building a helicopter, for example, you'll sometimes need to travel to the test facility (unless the test facility is across the street). This means, if the test facility is out of state, you will be traveling out of state for the tests. Not every job has the same amount of travel, so it's important that you are fully informed before you agree to a position.

Generally speaking, you're going to interact with people all over the country, so learn how to track tasks, communicate with team members in different ways (email, video call, team message, travel/in-person, etc.) You'll have to learn how to coordinate multiple time zones while scheduling video calls so nothing falls through the cracks. If your team members are away (or you're traveling) and you don't keep in mind you're working from different locations, it can be very easy to schedule a video call for a time that won't work. Stay organized, be responsive, and pay attention to detail so you don't accidentally schedule calls at the wrong time.

Know When to Leave

How do you know when to leave? You may be thinking, "Wait, shouldn't I stay in the world of government contracting?" Yes—I'm not talking about leaving it completely, but about knowing when to leave a specific job, a specific manager, or a specific organization.

For the most part, this is a missed opportunity for people. The reasons why people refuse to move on are many: maybe they're comfortable with the person they work for, like the program they support, or feel happy where they are and don't want to learn something new. Everyone has their reasons, and if you're happy where you are, don't leave... but the world is always changing, bosses come and go, program funding waxes and wanes, and because of all these other factors, comfort and happiness are always a moving target.

You might start at a job you absolutely love. Over time, your boss could be replaced by someone you don't click with as well. Program cuts may require you to move to another project, so what was once rewarding work becomes a drudgery. In that case, you might happier in a position where you can learn a new skill or be challenged. Keep your eyes open to the world around you and ask yourself on a regular basis: "Is this still the best place for me?"

In other words, don't be a passenger in your life; be an active participant. Every year, take stock and consider the following:

- Job risk
- Risk of leaving
- Whom you work for
- How much you make
- Where your kids are in school
- How close you are to retirement
- Where you are in the contract cycle
- How you feel about the company culture
- Opportunities you have at your current company
- How the government is funding the requirements

You will decide what questions are important to you (feel free to add or take away from this list... it's just a starting point). The main goal is to be aware. If you fail to evaluate where you're at and where you want to be, your position could be taken away, leaving you scrambling for a new one to pay the bills and care for your family. Of course, no employer wants to see a good employee leave, but it's your job to minimize your personal risk. To build your brand, you may need get to know other companies and departments (more about growing your personal brand later).

Bottom line: trust if you're asking whether you still belong somewhere, you're asking it for a reason. Go find out the answer. Your employer might be able to help you find those answers, but you'll have to develop a relationship with them over time. Some companies are open and honest. They want what's best for you more than what's best for them. Other companies are more concerned about profits and deadlines, so they'll tell you what you want to hear so they can keep you on the hook for them. Learn about the company's reputation over time and make decisions based on what you know to be true about their trustworthiness.

Action Steps

Not one action step this time, but two!

1. **Write down how much travel you're willing to do, if any.** Do you prefer to travel only within the US, or are you okay with travel abroad? Make sure you have a specific idea of what you're looking for so you'll know what to ask next time you're offered a position.

2. **Make a list of what factors into your ideal workplace.** Return to it once a year. If your priorities have changed, rewrite your list and compare your current position to that.

SWOT ANALYSIS SHEET

STRENGTHS	WEAKNESSES

OPPORTUNITIES	THREATS

CHAPTER 7

Keep the Government Out of Trouble

"It's much easier to stay out of trouble now than to get out of trouble later."

— WARREN BUFFETT, FORBES MAGAZINE [19]

So far, we've built a good foundation, but if you can't keep the government off the front page of the Washington Post, you won't succeed. Here's a simple test to see whether your actions or inactions could get the government in trouble: if someone says, "This is going to be the top story of a major news outlet," ask yourself if that's good or bad. If it's good, you have nothing to worry about. If it's bad, you need to make sure it doesn't happen. It's your first duty to protect the government.

A Difficult Conversation

Protecting the government isn't always easy. I've had to say "no" before, and those conversations can put you in a risky position.

In my case, a person wanted to use one type of money to pay for something illegal to do. While there can be gray areas in the financial world, these funds were specifically set aside: the purpose for them was clear. I had to stand up and say "no" to the person, without any idea of what would happen to me and my job if I did. Thankfully, the person in charge saw I was willing to do the right thing and protect this other person from breaking the law. Even though my experience was a positive one (I gained the trust of my leaders for all time), it isn't always that way. There are no guarantees this conversation will go well, but you have to protect the government even if it puts you in a risky position.

The example above is "just about money," but what if it's your job to prepare Airworthiness Releases (AWRs)? In that case, the consequences of not keeping the government out of trouble could mean the difference between life and death. Pencil whipped reviews and tests could translate to fatal failures on the field.

Whether the failure is on the building side, the training side, or the maintenance side, it can be deadly to skip important processes. On the training side, the nation-wide US Army aviation stand-down in April 2023 was a direct result of aviator fatalities. These deaths were mostly caused by spacial disorientation experienced by undertrained aviators—aviators who hadn't gotten enough flight hours.[20] On the maintenance side, disaster was narrowly averted in June 2023 when a routine inspection of US Army equipment transported from Kuwait to Ukraine showed the equipment was not battle-worthy. This equipment was supposed to be maintained by a contractor, but the contractor didn't do the job, resulting in faulty equipment that would have cost the lives of soldiers. Though the repairs cost thousands of dollars, lives were saved because the receiving soldiers followed protocol by inspecting their equipment upon arrival. [21]

When you feel something isn't right, remember you're part of a team. No man is an island and there are people you can lean on for support. Your direct manager may not have the same niche or experience you do, but they should be able to validate your concerns or reach out to people who can help you make the decision. Remember, you support the government, but you work for a company. If you like working with the government customer, but don't have support from the company you work for, you may need to make the tough decision to leave. I've had to leave in the past because keeping the government out of trouble is a team effort, and with the wrong team, it's nearly impossible. It's better to leave than struggle without support.

Tips on How to Talk About Problems

If you've put everything you've learned into practice up to this point, you know how to see the big picture and bring problems, challenges, and road-blocks to the government's attention, thereby keeping the government out of trouble. Every office has its own set of challenges. Now you see them and you can point them out… but how do you do that?

As I said before (in chapter five), you shouldn't just complain about what's bothering you. The most productive way is to couple problems with solutions. Coming up with solutions is easy… the hard part is moving through multiple layers of the government to implement a solution, sifting through regulations to determine whether you can even implement the solution, and getting the solution in place quickly enough. (The government isn't known for its speed.)

What not to say	What to say instead
"The process sucks."	"I noticed it takes a long time to get these approvals. If I (insert suggestion here), will it speed things along?"
"This doesn't work."	"Can you tell me why we do it this way instead of (insert better solution here)?"
"This is garbage."	"I thought of a way to improve on (insert topic here). Do you have some time to discuss it?"
"This is going to create more work without addressing the need."	"What is the objective you want to reach by taking this approach?" (Listen to feedback and then offer something to better address the need.)

"This is duplicative."	"We could streamline this process by (insert idea here)."

When is a Problem Not a Problem?

Sometimes, what you see as a problem is nothing more than a difference of opinion about how to read a rule or regulation. Just because you and the next person don't agree on how to interpret them doesn't mean one of you is right and the other is wrong. Remember, the rules are written in a vague way on purpose. As long as the whole office or department is in agreement (and they're not breaking any laws or regulations by interpreting them that way), it's better to stick with the interpretation the entire office or department is using.

To give you an idea of a part of government support left open for interpretation by the government, let's look at three different documents: a Statement of Work (SOW), Statement of Objective (SOO), and a Performance Work Statement (PWS). Many people will stick to just one of these documents and use it for everything in the office based on the office template. They don't think about the different intent of each document. Are these people wrong? It's hard to say, because according to the U.S. General Services Administration's statements on use:

A SOW is typically used when the task is well-known and can be described in specific terms. Statement of Objective (SOO) and Performance Work Statement (PWS) emphasize performance-based concepts such as desired service outcomes and performance standards. Whereas PWS/SOO's establish high-level outcomes and objectives for performance and PWS' emphasize outcomes, desired results and objectives at a more detailed and measurable level, SOW's provide explicit statements of work direction for the contractor to follow. However, SOW's can also be found to contain references to desired performance outcomes, performance standards, and metrics, which is a preferred approach.[22]

Did you notice they used the word "typically" out the gate? This goes to show you the flexibility of some government rules, and your job history and knowledge will come into play when determining what's a true problem and what's a difference of opinion. If you're not the person who has the final say about how to interpret and implement a rule, you're going to have to find a way to understand why and deal with it.

One More Thing

As you grow in your government contractor or subcontractor role, you'll learn there are three kinds of problems in the government: real problems needing to be addressed to keep the government out of trouble, differences of opinion about rule interpretation needing to be handled the same way by everyone at the office, and problems you can address to make life easier or streamline processes at the office. For the last two, you can engage with the government to provide solutions, learn "the why," and discuss how practices can be changed or how to improve communication. If your leaders don't accept your suggestions, don't take it personally. You are there to help, not to make the final decision. As long as no one is breaking the law, do all you can to keep the peace.

SWOT ANALYSIS SHEET

STRENGTHS	WEAKNESSES

OPPORTUNITIES	THREATS

CHAPTER 8

General Communication

"Great things in business are never done by one person.
They're done by a team of people."

— STEVE JOBS, 60 MINUTES INTERVIEW IN 2003 [23]

Communication is key in our everyday lives, but though you can choose whom you welcome into your personal life and how you engage with them, you can't choose your coworkers. This makes communication in the workplace a unique challenge, which is why I've chosen to cover it over the next few chapters. Communication in work can make or break your career, and the ability to express your thoughts, emotions, and intentions in a positive and productive way fosters trust and connection.

That said, communication isn't totally up to you. It's a team effort. In the same way a football team needs to hear and understand the play and the actions they must take in order to execute it properly, you need to have a team that understands the overarching goal and see it through to completion. It's not going to work if the linebacker keeps trying to make plays like a quarterback, leaving the quarterback wide open to the other team's offensive line. (Yes, this is a joke.)

What is Communication?

People tend to simplify what communication really is. They say, "I told my team member to send the email" and think that's the end of it. But what you say and how it's received can be very different. People read their experiences into how they receive information, so it's vital to ask questions after giving instructions to ensure there's understanding.

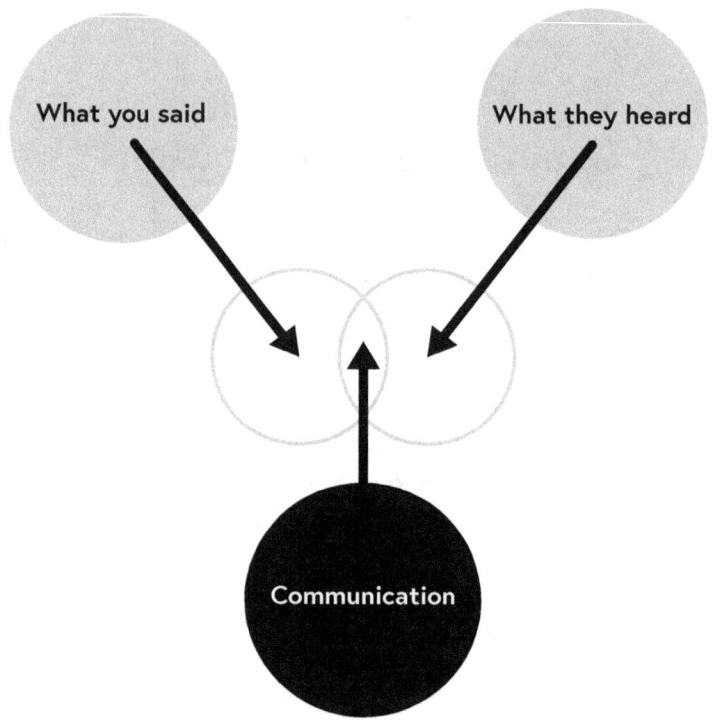

Communication is not as straightforward as you think—it's a result of what you said and what the other person heard

Telling a new team member to send an email without clarifying what tone it should have, how it should sound, whom should be copied into the email, etc. can be disastrous. You never want to micromanage a person, but if you've never communicated with them about what an email should look like before, you can't know for sure whether it'll be handled properly. If your team member's email winds up using the wrong tone, you'll be partly to blame for not talking to them about how to handle the issue in the first place.

Clarity in Communication

True communication is multi-layered. Communication should involve setting expectations and goals, ensuring you've got the right timing and audience, and being careful not to assume anyone has the same information you do.

Here's what I mean. When I owned a rental house, I noticed the flower beds in the front required a lot of maintenance. To make the house's upkeep easier, I asked a company to take it from mulch and flowers to rocks. I assumed they would know I wanted to prevent weeds from entering the flower beds, but I was wrong. The beds were taken down to the dirt, and rocks were placed on top with no weed barrier. I should have been crystal clear upfront. I could have asked about what specific materials they were going to use when I saw "labor and materials" listed on the estimate. They could have communicated to me the estimate didn't include the cost of a weed barrier, and if I wanted it, it would cost extra. A mutual failure to communicate led to a problem that didn't need to happen.

Agreement is not the same as understanding. A teammate might say, "Sure, I'll do it!" and have no idea how to do it. Most good coworkers ask for clarification, but some don't—they'll try to work it out on their own, in the dark, only to bring you something that doesn't check the boxes of what the final product should look like.

As an employee, it's up to you to engage as much as possible with those who provide you with tasks. You should be asking questions to gain a better understanding of what is expected of you, how your outcome will impact the team, and whether you can make the process more efficient. You are not acting alone—your piece of the task will go down the line to other team members—so make sure you're communicating clearly when you request your coworkers perform a specific task, and welcome them to ask questions.

The One "Yeah, but…" Rule

I created this rule long ago, when I realized my job is to help the government—nothing else. It's our job to create the most accurate, appropriate information or action as possible based on our information. It's then the government's job to plot the course for the path ahead. Often, people will do things that make no sense to us. In those moments, you get to say one time: "Yeah, but… (if you do this, this is what will probably happen)." Once you've done that, let the government make the decision and support it to the best of your ability.

Imagine you're on the radio with a guy flying in a helicopter above you. If you're standing on a corner and he says, "Go right," it's okay to say, "Yeah, but I go left because it's faster." That's the best path based on your view and your experience… but what if you don't have all the information? Maybe the guy will tell you, "An accident happened on that road, and it'll take you twice as long to get there." Now you know the person above you has more knowledge and a better view of the available paths, and they make decisions based on that. Not every leader says "go right" for the right reasons—sometimes they just want to go right—but it's your job to support good and bad communicators.

On Communication Styles

Not everyone communicates the same way. Some prefer written communication, and others would rather verbalize their communications to get things done as quickly as possible. The most considerate way to handle communication is to learn everyone's preferred communication styles and use their preferred styles as much as possible.

There are many benefits to discovering and using preferred communication styles, including:
1. You make your coworker feel heard and understood by meeting them halfway

2. You prevent them from communicating in a way they find uncomfortable

3. You increase the chances of them communicating more frequently with you

Not sure how to find out what communication style someone prefers? Just ask. It's as simple as, "Do you prefer I stop by your office when I have the report ready, or would you like me to email it to you?" In later communications, you can say something like, "I plan to stop by your office to deliver my report since that worked best for you last time, but let me know if you would prefer it via email today."

Generally speaking, people tend to have a favorite communication style across the board, but in some instances (such as a time crunch), they may prefer a more direct form of communication than they would typically use.

How you approach communication is also important. Will you take a leadership role or act as a follower? Some people don't see the value in taking action until you convince them it's what they want to do—it's got to feel like their idea. Some people are rule-followers and are resistant until you lay the rules out in front of them and explain the logic behind a certain course of action.

What to Do if Someone Takes Credit for Your Work

If someone has taken credit for your work, you've got three options. The one you take will depend on your knowledge of the person you're working with:

1. **Directly ask the person to correct the perception with leadership.** Choose this option if the event seemed like an honest mistake or the person who received credit appears awkward about the situation. Chances are, it was an accident, and they would be happy to clear it up with leadership.

2. **Backdoor effort: send your work history and communications to leadership.** Choose this option if you feel your fellow employee will only get angry or seems to enjoy taking credit for things they didn't do. Chances are, they won't act in good faith anyway, and this approach might prevent them from taking credit in the future.

3. **Do nothing this time, but resolve to get credit going forward.** Choose this option if you don't know the person well and probably won't work with them often anyway. In the future, jot a quick note to your boss about what you're working on with the other person before the employee sends the finished product.

Action Step

Write out the communication styles and preferences of the people you work with everyday. (If you like creating spreadsheets, go to town.) Keep this communication reference nearby so you can refer to it whenever you need to.

REMEMBER

Communication in work can make or break your career, and the ability to express your thoughts, emotions, and intentions in a positive and productive way fosters trust and connection.

SWOT ANALYSIS SHEET

STRENGTHS	WEAKNESSES

OPPORTUNITIES	THREATS

CHAPTER 9

Live and in Living Communication

"It's not just what you say but how you say it."

— ATTRIBUTED TO ALBERT MEHRABIAN, SILENT MESSAGES [24]

Live communication includes verbal and non-verbal communication, and can be the trickiest form of communication because it requires you to think on your feet and keep your facial expressions under control. (Not easy to do if you're feeling annoyed.) Organizing your thoughts when someone brings up a question you didn't expect can be hard, and not everyone is born a gifted speaker who can get straight to the point. Talking to another person in the moment comes with as many benefits as it does drawbacks.

Benefits of Live Communication

Live communication allows you to use your words, inflection, gestures, facial expressions, and tone to deliver a message. In many cases, it is the clearest and simplest form of communication there is. For example, if you're joking around with your best friend, they're not likely to be insulted. However, if you wrote the same things down and sent them in an email, your friend might think you're being cruel. How can the same sentence be perceived so differently? Because in live communication, you're using everything at your disposal to convey you're not serious... with exaggerated facial expressions, big movements, and a completely different tone of voice. You're also watching the person you're talking to—seeing how they take what you're saying in real time—to ensure they understand the joke.

These are the benefits of live communication:

- Quick and efficient
- Often more personable
- Uses verbal and nonverbal communication
- Instant feedback from the person you're talking to
- Can use active listening by repeating back what was said

Drawbacks of Live Communication

Live communication does present challenges, however. When there is a time constraint, it can sometimes be difficult to keep the conversation concise. Communication sometimes leads to "rabbit trails..." after all, the person you're communicating with might have a different agenda or topic in mind when you sit down to have a conversation with them. Another drawback is your body language often happens independently from your actual words and can betray your true feelings (even if you want to keep the peace and prevent the other person from knowing your true feelings). Those who understand body language cues may pick up on yours and call you out on it, which could lead to an uncomfortable conversation, especially if you're in the middle of a workplace conflict.

These are the drawbacks of live communication:

- Increased chance of "rabbit trails"
- Harder to document or record conversations
- Very difficult to control nonverbal cues during conflict
- Forgetfulness (either forgetting what they said or forgetting to mention something)
- Body language could lead to greater conflict in communication

Examples of Live Communication Challenges

Words matter, and unfortunately, they're easy for people to trip over. From 2011 to 2018, I was working for the Missile Defense Agency (MDA), and some of my tasks were to create policies, offer training, and answer questions about Intra/Inter-Agency Agreements (also called Support Agreements). There are many rules directly related to these agreements, including DoD Instruction 4000.19, 31 U.S.C. § 3521 **"Audits by Agencies,"** **31 U.S.C. § 1501 "Documentary Evidence Required for Government Obligations," DoD 7000.14-R "Financial Management Regulation," and more. These rules use the term "reimbursable support," and in these instances, the term refers to the exchange of money from one place to another. However, in other areas of the government, "reimbursable" has a dramatically different meaning—in fact, there are two types of funding: reimbursable and direct cite funding.**

This leads to a lot of confusion. During my time at the MDA, people told me the rules didn't apply to direct cite funds (which are the most commonly used funding type for contracts), and refused to use Support Agreements since the funds weren't being sent in a reimbursable fashion. I got into several heated discussions with people who told me I obviously didn't know how to read and didn't know what I was doing. They said I was creating unnecessary work because I wanted to justify my job, and wasn't able to see when a requirement didn't apply.

What it came down to was it's hard to change someone's mind when they've already formed an opinion, especially when you use a word that already has a specific definition in their minds. It's been a long time since I provided that support, and since then, the government has expanded information about the intent of Support Agreements, but even with the added clarity, I still see pushback today about whether people need to use a Support Agreement. To me, this shows some people want to cross the finish line as quickly as possible and don't care about the rules you need to follow to get there.

Another controversy over words erupted during a training on Support Agreement processes and policies in the same role at the MDA in 2015. On June 6, 2008, Paul A. Dennett had released a 70-page memorandum on "Improving the Management and Use of Interagency Acquisitions." The intent was to provide guidance on the rules for support agreements, including what agencies were, how they interacted, and what drove agency relationships.[25] Despite the government's efforts to provide clarity, this also led to a lot of confusion. This time, the word "acquisition" was the point of contention. (To be fair, there was a section stating the memo wasn't driven by the Federal Acquisition Regulations, or FAR, but for that to matter, people would have to read and understand it... and most people don't.)

During the training, a person in the group thought he was smarter than the entire policy group who'd spent months researching the requirement, talking with the authors, and determining how to communicate the requirements to the workforce. Instead of accepting the training as given, he wanted to show off his intelligence by asking, "What is the definition of 'acquisition'?"

Though I knew where he was going, I said, "Why don't you enlighten us?"

He began with, "Per the FAR," then recited the definition (which, just so you know, is):

> "Acquisition means the acquiring by contract with appropriated funds of supplies or services (including construction) by and for the use of the Federal Government through purchase or lease, whether the supplies or services are already in existence or must be created, developed, demonstrated, and evaluated. Acquisition begins at the point when agency needs are established and includes the description of requirements to satisfy agency needs, solicitation and selection of sources, award of contracts, contract financing, contract performance, contract administration, and those technical and management functions directly related to the process of fulfilling agency needs by contract." [26]

I was ready to go into attack mode, to tell him this wasn't appropriate to the training since support agreements aren't bound by the rules of the FAR, but before I could, his boss intervened. In a calm and professional way, the boss said, "Clearly the policy team knows the definition, but your question is irrelevant. This training has been researched, reviewed, and approved by the director of the agency. If he's approved it, it's appropriate to follow it."

Coming from him, the words were heavier than mine would have been, which was yet another group of lessons to me: words matter. Perspective matters. The seat in which you sit and how you engage with the work matters. Don't just present a topic or training from your lens—consider other viewpoints and cut off any miscommunication issues that can arise before they happen.

One More Thing

If I would have taken some additional time to think about how the training would be received, how the workforce viewed the words in the training, and the definitions of those words, I could have started the training differently. Today, I would have opened the training with the history of the requirement, how the various pieces of it fit together, and a language road map to show how each word's meaning may be different than expected. Would I capture everything, cut off all dissent? No, but I would show the other side's thoughts and show those thoughts were considered upfront instead of opening a path to conflict.

SWOT ANALYSIS SHEET

STRENGTHS	WEAKNESSES

OPPORTUNITIES	THREATS

CHAPTER 10

Written Communication

"The difference between the almost right word and the right word is… the difference between the lightning bug and the lightning."

— MARK TWAIN, THE ART OF AUTHORSHIP [27]

Written communication gives you more time to draft a response, but it's harder to convey the tone. It typically takes more time and is more formal than verbal communication. While written communication may be the last communication type an extrovert wants to participate in, it may strike introverts as a communication form ripe with benefits.

Benefits of Written Communication

Written communication provides an opportunity to visually organize your thoughts. While a TL:DR; (Too Long, Didn't Read;) wouldn't make sense in a verbal context, it's perfectly appropriate for a written email or document. There are other ways to create a visual hierarchy in your communication, such as the use of bold or italicized words to draw attention to main points, or the use of bullet points or numbered lists to ensure nothing is missed in a list of instructions. For example, this book is a piece of written communication, and in it I've made use of paragraph breaks, headings, bolded words, italics, and bullet point lists to help convey my meaning. In a verbal message, thoughts tend to flow together, and it can be difficult to organize them (for example, when creating a transcript of an audio file or podcast).

Here are the benefits of written communication:

- Provide a visual hierarchy to show items of importance
- Ideal for introverts or those who struggle to verbally organize thoughts
- More time to respond to new information (parties respond when convenient)
- Physical evidence of what was said (ability to review communications before sending)
- Easier to come across in a composed or professional way

Drawbacks of Written Communication

There are some drawbacks to written communication, however. When there is a need for an urgent response, it's wiser to respond in person. Also, it's sometimes considered impolite, unprofessional, or cowardly to respond via written communication when verbal communication (face-to-face) would be a better option. For example, when there is a public relations issue, as in the case of a national security issue, etc., it is best to make a statement verbally, even if you are reading aloud a prepared statement.

The drawbacks of written communication include:

- Tone is difficult to distinguish
- Takes longer than verbal or live communication
- Can take a long time to read or appears less interesting
- Can appear disingenuous, etc., especially when live communication is appropriate
- Unstructured written communication is nearly impossible to get feedback on

Examples of Written Communication Challenges

When I was young and in my first year of government support in 2007, I wrote an email—an email I didn't notice was in all caps—and it did not go well. You may be wondering, "How could you not know the email was in all caps?" I'll tell you: I saw an email come in, hit reply, and when the box opened, I put it behind a document I was referencing for the response. I just typed, not seeing what I was typing, finished the email, and hit send. I didn't even look at what I wrote after I sent it off. Less than five minutes later, I was pulled into my manager's office with the person I responded to. The manager immediately asked, "What the F*** is your problem?"

Needless to say, this was the beginning of the end for me at that job. My response was simple: "I don't know what you are talking about…"

The manager brought the email up on her computer, but I still couldn't see it since I was on the other side of the desk. They said, "This is the email you sent."

This email content was pretty simple, it just referenced some regulations about how to do what I was being asked about. Without all caps, it was fine. In all caps it was angry, condescending and flat out rude. But I still didn't see the email, so I said, "What's wrong with it? It is right."

The email recipient said, "So you think I am stupid, then?"

I was a bit shocked and didn't exactly know what to think or how to respond (probably because I did think the person was stupid, but how she got that from an email I was at a loss over). So I just said, "No."

Both of them looked at me with the fire of a thousand suns in their eyes and told me to leave, so I did. I went back to my desk, opened the email, and saw it was in all caps. I finally understood what happened, but instead of going back in and addressing it, I just waited for them to re-engage, and they never did. A lot of things were wrong with this situation: I was lazy by not validating what I was sending, then was shocked in the moment instead of asking a valid question. I didn't engage to figure out why they were really mad, and I didn't walk right back in once I saw the FUBAR nature of the email because I was too frustrated at myself for sending it in all caps. I probably did a ton of other things wrong I can't articulate to this day. This moment destroyed my relationship in the office with two people (one of whom was a manager), and within a few weeks, I quit to leave a bad situation and finish my masters degree. Was it the right choice? Maybe, maybe not. But it was the choice I made at the time. I could see the writing on the wall and decided quitting was better than being fired.

This is an extreme situation. It started with poor written communication, then turned into poor verbal communication, and finally ended with no communication. But through it, you can see how one moment can change everything.

Another common error is assuming communication means someone will act. If you want to see positive action, start by making people want to help you. Assigning people tasks when you don't have the power to do so or when they don't actually want to help is not going to get the job done. This is why it's better to find out a person's communication style and maintain a good relationship them before you ask for help.

Here are few more quick examples of what can go wrong in written communications:
- Being too long-winded
- Forgetting to spell-check
- Being ambiguous about the point of the email
- Sending an email but forgetting the attachment
- Using acronyms or verbiage the recipient doesn't know
- Putting together an email when a quicker response is necessary
- Not giving a deadline when you need a deliverable by a certain date or time
- Adding too many exclamation points to an email (this make you seem unprofessional)
- Responding to an email while emotional (instead, write it, walk away, rewrite, then send)
- Not saying why you need a deliverable or who told you to do the task (sometimes giving a person this information will help you get an answer quicker)

Written Communication Guidelines for Government Contractors

#1: Choose one topic per email. I have seen so many 500-word emails with 10 topics. Guess what—no one reads them. If something is important, send it on its own. Many times, I have seen random stuff in emails with a specific request buried halfway down a page. Often, the sender is shocked when no one responds to their request. This won't happen if you send one topic per email.

Adding more than one topic per email can become very confusing, especially when your email has to pass through several hands before the topic is resolved. How can anyone track, manage, and find the history of a topic when it's buried in the fourth paragraph of an email with a subject line about "training" but is asking a question about a template for a document? Getting 300 emails a day isn't ideal, but it's better than having a completely disorganized and untrackable system.

On a related note, if you're asking for several days off work, you should send one email per request instead of putting them all in the same one. You might think putting them all together is a time saver, but remember, you're just level one, and a request needs to travel through multiple levels (manager, travel coordinator, contracts, finance, government) in order to be approved. Each trip must be reviewed and submitted individually, so multiple requests in one email can create confusion down the road.

#2: Match the email title and body. Make sure the title of the email matches the topic in the body of the email. People scan emails, then save them. When they think about the email again, they'll search for it based on its topic, not the title.

#3: Document everything. You know the saying: "If it's not on video, it didn't happen." Well, in the government, if it's not documented, it didn't happen. After a conversation, phone call, meeting, or any other form of conversation you'll need to lean on in the future, immediately send a recap via email. (This is also called the "per our conversation" email.) The goal is to create a history you can refer to, and ideally, you'll get a response from the other person as well, to solidify the conversation or clear up misunderstandings.

Beyond the obvious (creating a written history of important conversations), this serves as a memory jogger in case you forget some of the nuances about what was discussed. (Note: documenting a conversation doesn't mean it's now written in stone and impossible to change... you're just documenting where you are at currently. You are welcome to change things if needed, but now you'll have a record of how they changed along the way.)

REMEMBER

In the government, if it's not documented, it didn't happen.

SWOT ANALYSIS SHEET

STRENGTHS	WEAKNESSES

OPPORTUNITIES	THREATS

CHAPTER 11

Grow Your Brand

"Personal branding is all about your unique promise of value and what you bring to the table. It's (also) about getting your potential clients to choose you as the only solution to their problem."

— DR. SARAH DAVID, ALL THINGS TALENT MAGAZINE [28]

Once you know the basics, growing your brand is the most important part of being a successful government support contractor. You might be wondering: why is it so important? First, let me give you some reminders.

If you work in government support, you do not work for the government. You work to support the government, which means you work for the company that holds the contract with the government. Here's the thing: contracts for support staff terminate about every five years, so if the company wins the contract again, you'll keep working like nothing happened. However, if they don't win the contract, what happens to you will depend on how well you've grown your brand. They can try to keep you on at the company by moving you to another office, or (if they don't like you or your work), they can let the contract lapse and make no effort to keep you.

If you've done a good job of creating, maintaining, and growing your brand, your options will be good even if the company you're currently with loses the contract. You can work at a new office with the same company (since they'll do all they can to find you another contract so you'll continue on as their employee), or you can seek employment with the new company that earned the contract. (If you've created a strong name for yourself as a smart, capable teammate, the government office will do everything they can legally do to keep you.)

Your Brand: A Complete Package

If you're not sure what a brand is, it's a complete package including:
- How well you do your job
- How knowledgeable you are
- How well-liked you are
- The boxes you've checked on your resume

Getting in the door is a major accomplishment, but you won't stay there unless you keep yourself relevant by attending training, sharpening your skills, studying, and honing your craft. Growing your brand in this way also helps with job security. Many people prefer not to go into government support contracting because of job instability. "Who would want to work in that field when it could mean a job change every five years?" I get it—since I started this work in 2007, eight different companies have paid my salary.

I worked:
- As a government intern supporting the US Army
- As an intern at Lockheed-Martin
- At a company supporting RDECOM (Research, Development, and Engineering Command)
- At two companies supporting the MDA (Missile Defense Agency)
- At two companies supporting the PEO (Program Executive Office) Aviation for the Army
- At a company supporting the FBI (Federal Bureau of Investigation)

Guess what—through all the churn and change, I never felt like my job was unstable because of the system. I had stability because I built a solid brand and committed to growth even after I got in the door. At one point, I was a senior-level acquisitions analyst and was going through a contract change. The original contract with the company only required a bachelor's degree and eight years of experience to qualify, but the new contract increased the education requirement to a master's degree with eight years of experience. Because I decided to continue my education and obtain a master's, I was able to keep my senior status, but not all analysts were so lucky—some had stopped at their bachelor's and needed to apply at the journeyman level (or seek another job altogether).

If you're consistently able to make someone's work life easier, you're succeeding at building your brand. One of my favorite comments to hear from my team, my company, or the government customer I'm supporting is I've made their work easier. Make it your goal not only to get work done to meet the need but to do it quickly and correctly. Building a solid brand everywhere you go will pay off in ways you haven't even imagined yet. You won't be the only person in government support to move jobs—most people spend an average of three years in the same position.

Building a strong professional relationship within your office today may get you a foot in the door when someone who works there is in a new office later on. I remember when I left the internship with the Army to finish my MBA. Though a lot of that experience was terrible—horribly terrible— I didn't realize many people saw I was capable and would not just be a yes man. They saw I was learning the craft, knew the rules, and had their backs. I was able to go work for the company that supported RDECOM later because of a person I worked with during the Army job who knew me and wanted me on his team. I would not have even known about the RDECOM opportunity had it not been for this person.

If you want to travel the world, you may get to do it because of the opportunities your branding gives you.

How to Grow Your Brand

Now you know the advantages of growing your brand, but how do you do it? Here are some of the mindset shifts that need to happen before you start.

1. **Realize you're not going to get along with everyone.** Hey, I'm a realist: there's just no way you're going to like everyone you come in contact with, and even if you do, they won't all like you. Some personalities won't mesh well with others. Don't ignore this fact—you can overcome it. I've worked with many people who can't stand my personality but know the work I put forth is high-quality, follows regulations, and helps us meet our end goals. We won't grab a beer after work to watch the game, but we still work well together in a professional sense. This took me a lot of learning and practice to figure out. Believe me, it was not a skill in the beginning of my career.

2. **Know your branding goal is to gain professional respect.** Don't try to grow a brand by being someone you're not. It's dishonest and people can tell it from a mile away. Strive to always be genuine, honest, and open enough not to cause tension that will harm your brand. The goal is to prove your competence and earn respect.

3. **Be aware your brand is constantly changing.** Every day you go to the office, you either increase or decrease your brand's reputation. To increase your reputation, you can keep beefing up your resume by ensuring the boxes are checked for your background, experience, education, skills, reference contacts, etc. You can also kill your brand by refusing to be a team player, not knowing the rules and regulations, bringing down the office with a negative or confrontational attitude, or forgettingone of your main purposes is to keep the government out of trouble.

Now that you've got your mindset in the right place, here's what you need to do to grow your brand:

- **Learn.** Every day is an opportunity to learn something new. Get curious and explore. Learning about the world around you (and the work itself) is a big part of becoming a well-rounded person.
- **Help people (even if they take credit).** If someone takes credit for your work, it sucks, but don't let it discourage you from helping

someone else. (In the next chapter, learn what to do if someone takes credit.)

- **Refuse to take credit for someone else's work.** This is the flip side of the one above. Don't take credit for work you didn't do! If a supervisor asks about collaborative work, be honest about everyone's contributions.
- **Show up every day.** No, this doesn't mean never taking a sick day. It means on the days you work, you should do all you can to be positive, supportive, and productive. (If you are sick, take a sick day. You should take vacations, too!)
- **Be a team player.** Have you ever worked with someone who loves doing the bare minimum and never wants to contribute? It sucks. As much as you can (without crossing the line of your job description's parameters), be a team player.
- **Solve problems.** It's a lot easier to spot a problem than it is to solve it, but that's why problem-solvers stand out: while everyone else is complaining about the issue, they find and implement solutions.
- **Be prepared—things will go wrong.** You can't know when everything's going to fall apart, but you can be ready for it. Follow my organizational tips to ensure you're ready with the documentation you'll need when the moment arises.

Finally, act with purpose. Think about what you're about to do—whether you want to question a decision, provide suggestions on what path to take, or add input on a topic—and look at it from every angle. Think of how the person could take it. Are you okay with that response? Can you soften the person's reaction by changing your approach or defuse the situation if it gets hostile? Remember, what you say, you can't un-say.

How to act with purpose:

- **Understand whom you're engaging with.** Are they receptive, or are they know-it-alls who'll be offended no matter what you say because they think a question is an attack on their ability to do their jobs? This takes time to learn, but the goal should be to engage with people who roll with the punches, are technically capable, and have a positive view.

- **See the battlefield.** Visualize the options laid out in front of you and plan your approach. (This step is informed by step one, and will determine whether the response from leadership is, "Yeah, let's do that," "Yeah, but…," "You're an idiot," or something more aggressive.)
- **Act.** Don't just sit on an email, a task, or a request for information. Act with intelligence, knowing what to expect because of steps one and two. After you've acted, don't take the response personally—just let it inform you next time. Be ready for pushback (or a screamfest). Some people can take criticism from several people well, but yours ends up being the straw that broke the camel's back.
- **Learn (continually).** The cycle of communication is always in motion because life is never stationary. Maybe Greg at the office is always mild-mannered, but now he's going through a heartbreaking divorce. Maybe he's got a new baby and hasn't slept in three days. Maybe his best friend just got in a car accident. Be ready to change how you respond to people, because people will change.

One More Thing
"Leave it better than you found it."

This advice is great in general, but especially helpful when it comes to work. You will not stay in a position forever… that's the nature of government support. You learn, grow, and work in a new place more interesting to you, but if you make the place you're currently at better, you'll create a stronger brand for yourself. Use your imagination, but some ways to do this are to pay attention to the processes you follow, write down the steps you take to do a task, create a manual about your job, or come up with a faster way of doing something. Not only will you be helping the team you're working with and the next person in your role, but you'll build a great reputation for yourself.

REMEMBER

Once you know the basics,
growing your brand is the
most important part of being a
successful government
support contractor.

SWOT ANALYSIS SHEET

STRENGTHS	WEAKNESSES

OPPORTUNITIES	THREATS

CHAPTER 12

Grow Your Career

"There is no passion to be found playing small—in settling for a life that is less than the one you are capable of living."

— ATTRIBUTED TO NELSON MANDELA BY DENZEL WASHINGTON AT PENN [29]

How do you talk to your boss about something you need? It's a struggle for many people, and there's a lot of nervousness about how to ask about gaining more experience, more work, more pay, or more travel. Here's my take: just ask! Don't wait for your team lead, manager, or company owner to read your mind or grant permission for you to do what you want. Sometimes the next step will naturally come to you, but more often than not, you have to ask for it. Hope is not a plan—don't wait around for someone to notice you.

Even if you ask, there's no guarantee you'll get a "yes" response. Sometimes this is beyond your boss' control: there's nothing available. Sometimes you're working at a greedy company that doesn't want to give you a raise. Sometimes you're not ready for the next step. Sometimes there are factors at play you haven't even considered yet.

Once you have an answer, determine your path ahead based on the conversation. Only you can decide what to do next. Your sense of worth is personal—you've got to do what feels right for you. At times, I've had people at the top of their pay scale ask me for a raise, and I had to tell them I couldn't do that, but we're always looking for new contracts, and if we secure one, we could see about moving them to the contract with higher rates. These same people have asked the owner, too, and they got the same response. Some left for other jobs feeling they were not being told the truth, while others stayed knowing we were doing all we could.

Working on a Government Contract

Government contracts have each position's rates built into them. This may seem straightforward but it has more consequences than you might think. First, there are overhead costs that need to be accounted for within the price of the contract. Second, because the competition is fierce, companies sometimes bid low rates in a "race to the bottom" in the hopes of winning a contract. If a company has used that strategy to win a contract and you were already working in the office, you'd be lucky to keep the same salary you had before. It's not always the case: sometimes people need to take a lower pay rate to stay at the same office.

Allow me to dispel a myth about escalations, too—just because a company has a 2.5% year-over-year escalation built into its contract doesn't mean you're going to get a raise, and if you do, it's probably not going to be a 2.5% raise. It's highly likely the company sees it differently than you do.

Here's a breakdown of what they could be envisioning:
- Years one and two go toward overhead
- Year three helps us break even
- Years four and five, we finally earn a profit (maybe)

Those at the top of the rate table can go five years without a pay raise—I know this because I've seen it and I've experienced it myself. You've got to decide how to handle this. Do you need frequent raises? If so, how do you plan to accomplish it within the government support world? Learn the contract and the labor categories, and don't forget to ask questions about the ability to get raises in the future through LCAT growth.

Growth Takes Time

Don't expect to grow overnight, but remember there's not a lot of mobility built into government support. You've got a specific job to do, and unless you *ask*, you could end up in a niche where you're not adding value or growing in experience. Remember, comfort is the enemy of growth, and being comfortable in one spot is usually not a good sign you're learning.

Help people in other career fields, learn to grow in yours, and be willing to change career fields. Work with all kinds of people so you can learn how to communicate with those of different temperaments and personalities. The jobs that typically increase pay over time require lots of communication, interaction, and engagement. Building solid professional relationships will help you get there quicker.

As your career grows, don't forget to add to your resume. One element that can round out your resume is to feature awards and recognition you've gotten over the years. Not every culture will want to hand out awards, which is okay. Some places I've worked gave awards out like candy, and others refused to do so because people were using them to arguethey deserved a higher CPARS (Contractor Performance Assessment Rating System) score. If you're getting awards and recognition, be sure to document them in your resume.

When People Take Credit for Your Work

We all want recognition, right? It feels nice to know people see what we're doing…but when other people take credit for our ideas, it's hard to stay calm (especially when we see them accepting opportunities they wouldn't have without our contributions). The way I see it, you've got three choices about how to respond when someone takes credit for your work, and as I said in the last chapter, you'll have to factor in what you know about the person to make the right choice.

You can:

- **Confront the person taking credit and ask them to clear it up with leadership.** If it seemed like a fluke or you know the person who took credit is basically honest and they seemed about as awkward about the recognition as you did, this approach should work. Have an open and honest discussion, and ask them to have a chat with leadership about your contributions.

- **Take the "backdoor" approach by showing leadership the history.** If you know the person who took credit is combative, angry, or has a bad habit of taking credit for other people's work, this might be the best approach to take. Don't bother going to the person who took credit—instead, go directly to your leader and show them the history of your conversations or contributions. This way, you're being open and honest about the work you did while avoiding a confrontation with a coworker.

- **Deal with the loss this time and learn how to get credit going forward.** If you don't work with the other person often, are not sure how they'll react, or if it's a first-time offense, you can take the loss today and plan to get credit next time. One way to ensure you get credit for the next project is to send your lead a quick note or email saying what you're working on before your coworker has a chance to send the finished product.

Note: Not everyone's going to want to "take the loss," even for a first-time offense. It's frustrating to know someone took credit for your work, so if your personality won't allow you to continue working alongside someone who's taken credit (while keeping things on an even keel), it's probably best you choose one of the first two options instead.

Be Open to Change

It's not 1950—you won't work for the same company your whole career. The average person in this line of work moves companies regularly. Be open to opportunities and growth. Think about where you want your life to be five, 10, 15, and 20 years from now. Create a roadmap to meet those goals. If you need more education, relationships, or travel time to make them happen, add them to your plan for the path forward.

Another area to watch out for in terms of stagnation is projects. If you're not careful, you could end up on the same types of projects (ones with similar timelines, expectations, etc.). Be adventurous and take on different kinds of projects: detailed long-term projects requiring steady progress and fast-paced projects with aggressive schedules. This will enable you to become more flexible and give you an idea of what kinds of projects you prefer most.

I've worked all over the place in government support:
- As an intern in contracts, supporting the US Army
- Working in the contracts shop for the FBI
- As an acquisition analyst, a program integrator, and a policy analyst at MDA
- As a financial analyst, supporting the Apache helicopter at PEO Aviation
- As a financial analyst, supporting the F-35 Lightning II at Lockheed-Martin

I've had positions in:
- Florida
- Colorado
- Alabama
- Washington DC
- Virginia

I've traveled all over the world for my work—to meet with clients or stake-holders. Sometimes I took jobs because I was leaving a bad environment, and sometimes it was to get the next level of seniority (or higher pay). The point is not to sit in the same seat forever—look around, see the world, and grow as a person and in your career.

On Burning Bridges

They say "Never burn a bridge," but the truth is you are only able to control your side of the bridge. After you've done everything you can to make your parting as friendly and professional as possible, the other party may choose to burn the bridge. Choices have consequences and people have emotions. Your decision to leave a company may negatively impact someone else—recognize that and move on.

Sometimes a burned bridge can be rebuilt (either after some time passes or because the affected person leaves the company). Never decide to stay somewhere because you may burn a bridge if you go. That said, you should be aware of the possibility a bridge could be burned and factor it into the decision-making process.

I knew one of the jobs I left would probably result in not being able to support that office anymore, and I still left. I felt the office didn't respect its employees. It was so stressful and unhealthy I didn't want to return anyway. I felt like I did my job and provided the highest level of support I could given the circumstances, but if I had to do it all over again, I still would have left that office. Always try not to burn a bridge, but if you do, continue to move forward.

REMEMBER

Don't expect to grow overnight, but remember there's not a lot of mobility built into government support. You've got a specific job to do, and unless you ask, you could end up in a niche where you're not adding value or growing in experience.

SWOT ANALYSIS SHEET

STRENGTHS	WEAKNESSES

OPPORTUNITIES	THREATS

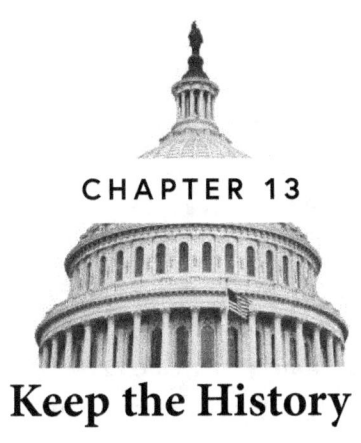

CHAPTER 13

Keep the History

"If you don't write it down, then it never happened."

— TOM CLANCY, DEBT OF HONOR [30]

I'm about to let you in on a government secret: almost nothing is done from scratch. All the documents we use, the drawings, the spreadsheets… they're all a version of a version from the past. It makes procedures more efficient (you're customizing what's worked before), but it also makes it a nightmare to manage the history. You've got to keep the versions that matter and wade through endless emails to find a note from months ago (after you've probably already forgotten the minute details).

There's a disconnect within the government as far as how records are kept. Record-keeping is required, but the government does it poorly. Unfortunately, the government is always changing operating systems (OS), storage systems, and file structures, making it hard to keep track of which record is where. (Is it on the old Sharepoint or the new one? Your guess is as good as mine!) To make matters worse, the government doesn't offer strong accountability or have set systems to ensure record-keeping is done properly. Even though the government does have many rules to govern records management,[31] record keeping is your responsibility. While this can seem like a heavy burden, it's also a major opportunity for you to set yourself apart and further build your brand.

Why Build a System to Keep the History?

Maybe you're thinking, "John, why go to all the trouble?" In short, you're going to need it:

- One day, someone will ask you to create a brief including information from something you created two years ago, and you'll need to quickly find the file (unless you enjoy rebuilding it all from scratch).

- One day, you're going to be asked why you did things a certain way (or you'll be asked who decided to do it that way) so you can write a history paper about how we got to where we are. Without a system, you'll look bad, because the person asking won't see the hundreds of "small tweaks" made to a contract over the years, and now it will look like it's overrunning.

- One day, the new head of a program will come in, and he or she will want a briefing about all the changes and the history of the contract. Without a system, this is going to mean many sleepless nights for you!

A benefit of building a record-keeping system is you look great—like you have all the answers—because anytime needs information, you can pull it up. The government has specific rules but loose processes, and as frustrating as not having set processes sounds, it's actually a benefit because you can adapt your process to what works best for you. When you tailor the process to your own organizational style, it helps you file and find what you need faster. This makes the work easier when you have to recall information down the line. You won't take as long to re-learn information because you won't have to sift through a mountain of emails to do it! This also protects you in the future if you need to go from a place with existing processes to a place where there are none. You'll be able to put your processes in place and build your brand in the new location.

Two sayings that go around in the government world are: "The output is only as good as the input" and "No one ever has enough time." Both of these problems are solved by diligent record-keeping. Organizing the record well prevents you from taking extra time to find crucial information, and you'll have all the input you need to achieve a great output.

Practical Organization Tips to Keep the History

If you're not sure where to start with keeping the history, I'm happy to let you in on what I do. If it works for you, great! If it doesn't, find something else that will work (keeping in mind file formats and operating systems change often within the government).

Tip #1: Create folders and subfolders to organize information.

How it works:

Got an email you're going to have to refer to later? I classify my emails under one of two categories. The ones requiring action from me are "Active" tasks and the ones not requiring action from me are "Closed" tasks.

1. I create folders and subfolders (by topic) for all "Closed" tasks. That way, I can refer to them quickly when writing briefs, etc. Examples: I add my history about creating a Statement of Work (SOW), Military Interdepartmental Purchase Requests (MIPR), etc. in these folders.

2. I keep my "Active" tasks in my inbox, but I tag them (using a red flag in Outlook) so I know exactly which emails need my attention. Examples: a topic that could be important for a brief, a story, or a whitepaper stays in my inbox with a red flag.

3. If a new email comes in to take the place of the previously tagged one, I move the tag over to the new email so I've always got the latest information. Doing this ensures I always see the most up-to-

date information when I'm looking at my inbox, and those tasks don't get lost.

This way of organizing won't work for everyone, but the benefit of this system is you have an archive of information while also honing in on the most relevant or recent messages quickly.

Note: if any of these emails are digitally signed, save them as PDFs and then keep the PDFs. Often, once you get new credentials in your email, you won't be able to open past signed emails because the system won't recognize the new CAC certification.

Tip #2: Create a personal shared drive or SharePoint location.

How it works:

Trying to keep every piece of important information would result in a lot of needless paperwork and duplication. No one wants that, so don't use this system for forms saved elsewhere (like financial forms, etc.).

1. Create a personal share drive or SharePoint location (whether you go with a shared drive or SharePoint will depend on the work location). Use it to keep track of files that are always changing, like a Rough Order of Magnitude (ROM), Cost Estimate Document, or Statement of Work, because even though the final version and any updated versions should be included in the contract file, they aren't always saved and updated properly. Keeping a version of everything on the cloud will be a huge help if your computer dies.

2. Don't just keep the information you worked on, but document the process you're using to meet the requirements. The rationale for changes or exclusions is lost if you don't have the notes and comments on the working file, so I keep my own records for certain files just in case.

3. Note: Some commands don't like personal folders or pages, so you may not be able to do this everywhere.

As I said before, do what works for you… But please don't put 500 sticky notes on your computer screen.

Action Step

Try one (or both) of the tips I shared as a starting point to create your system. As you use it, check in regularly: is this working for you? Are there any tweaks you can make to create a more effective system—one that suits your personality or style better? Keep working on your systems to fine-tune it to your preferences.

SWOT ANALYSIS SHEET

STRENGTHS	WEAKNESSES

OPPORTUNITIES	THREATS

CHAPTER 14

Help Your Company

*"There are no great limits to growth because there are no
limits of human intelligence, imagination, and wonder."*

—RONALD REAGAN, 40TH US PRESIDENT

CONVOCATION CEREMONIES AT THE UNIVERSITY OF SOUTH

CAROLINA IN COLUMBIA [32]

Everything else in this book is exclusively about becoming a successful
contract employee—and that's important, but part of becoming a successful contract employee also involves helping your company. Some people
don't realize this, and it can negatively affect their careers even if they're
doing the rest of their job right.

There are several ways to help your company. Some ideas include everything from remembering to put in your timecard, to wearing the company logo, to showing up at the Christmas party. There's some leeway here:
obviously, you don't want to show up to the Christmas party sick, and
you might decide not to if you're grieving the death of a friend or family
member. That's perfectly understandable. Entering your timecard, though,
should be a given. If you need to set a reminder on your phone or in some
other way, do it. (We'll talk more about timecards later in this chapter.)

Why Help Your Company?

Helping your company comes with obvious benefits to the company itself.
It creates culture and togetherness within the company, keeps the company

accountable to its employees, and proves the company is capable, responsive, and engaged. Whether you help your company can determine the difference between whether it becomes well-known and established as a great place to work or not.

What you may not realize is helping your company will also be beneficial to you. Well-known companies get more teaming agreements to go after more work, which means more job opportunities and growth opportunities for you at the company. If you decide to apply to another company down the line, the company will look at your resume in a stronger light if you come from a high-level location with a reputation for fostering education, personal growth, and treating its employees well.

Helping your company won't take much extra time or commitment on your part—just a mindset shift. For example, you may think forgetting to fill out your timecard on time might not be a big deal, but it affects everyone. What you may not know is the systems used to complete timecards also typically run payroll. This means, potentially, the entire company's payroll can't be completed until all the timecards are submitted. Not completing your timecard could mean payroll is pushed back, and if payroll is pushed back, this could create accounting challenges, which could result in you (and your fellow employees) not being paid on time. For people living paycheck to paycheck, this is a huge deal. Even a paycheck that comes one day late can result in bill pay issues, overdraft fees, etc. This affects the company as well: imagine how hard it'd be to hire people if your company is known not to pay its employees on time.

This final point folds in on itself in several ways: helping your company enables you to hold the company accountable, and holding the company accountable is helpful to your company. Accountability is a major contributor to success. When a company is accountable to its employees, employees are more likely to take accountability. I've worked for a lot of different companies within government contracting—companies of different sizes, structures, leadership styles, etc., but the one character trait all successful companies have in common is accountability. A successful company follows through on its promises. It asks about the perspectives of its employees. Sometimes one person's perspective doesn't help solve the issue or there's more at play, so that person is told no, but the bottom line is good companies ask for feedback (and are still using the feedback to make big-picture decisions).

If something isn't working well within the company, you should speak up. Remember, the government contract world is always changing, and communication is critical for leadership to make good decisions to support the company. If you're having problems with policy, processes, benefits, etc., working together as a team is the best way to overcome those challenges.

How to Help Your Company

Here are the best ways I've found to help my company. Maybe these will help you too.

1. **Deliver quality work.** This is your first calling card, the first step in building your brand. The higher the caliber of your work, the more you elevate the company you work at, which can trickle downward and upward as you set a standard of excellence.

2. **Build and maintain strong relationships with the customer and the company.** Remember, the customer in this case is the government agency with which the company holds a contract, and the company is who signs your paychecks. Get an understanding of the customer's needs, including the specific requirements of your position and the customer's goals. Tailor your work to meet their expectations on an ongoing basis. Stay up-to-date with policy, regulation, and initiative changes that could impact your work or the company's objectives. Keep track of deadlines, budgets, and reporting requirements.

3. **Communicate clearly and consistently with internal teams and government customers.** We've covered communication, but you

can never have too much as long as you're doing it right. Regular updates and progress reports are essential. Act as the go-between for the government and your company. Ensuring your company knows what goes on at a government site will help the company know how to approach potential position growth or LCAT increases, which will help you and the company.

4. **Contribute to a positive company culture.** Support collaboration and teamwork within the company. Offer to mentor or assist less experienced colleagues, contributing to a learning environment benefiting everyone. Be a person others want to work around! This is a good question to ask yourself: Do my attitude and behavior make the government customer want me around?

5. **Don't forget about business development.** You don't have to be a capture manager or business development professional to write a section of a proposal talking about an area you specialize in. If you're knowledgeable in your field, you should offer to draft proposals because it'll help you become more well-known in the company while fostering growth in it. Support your company's efforts to win new contracts by contributing to proposals or identifying new opportunities. Stay engaged with the business development team to understand how you can support the company's growth.

6. **Be ethical.** Government contractors are held to high ethical standards. Advocate for transparency, fairness, and integrity in all dealings with the government and other contractors. If your company has an ethics or compliance team, engage with them regularly to ensure you know the latest regulations and practices. (In small companies, this would be the HR team.) By focusing on ethics, you'll help your company stand out as a reliable, competent, and innovative partner for the government.

I always look for ways to be better at my job, help the company grow, and build strong relationships, since my policy is helping the company will help me. I've seen this to be true through the promotions I've gotten over the years based on my willingness to go above and beyond to provide support, as well as my willingness to move around. I've helped by writing proposals, mentoring other employees, shutting up and coloring inside the lines when it was right to do so, and standing up and arguing when it was right to do so. These calls aren't always easy to make, but the more you do them, the more you'll get in return.

One time, I was at a baseball game on the Fourth of July when I got a phone call from the business development team from my company because the government released a Request for Proposal (RFP) on the third of July (before a "long weekend"). The government probably does this to encourage the company to enjoy its day off, and then work on the proposal when the holiday is over, but they don't realize that's not how contract companies work. The RFP comes out, and we immediately work on it. We read the requirements, schedule, and questions, and then start trying to build out our responses by giving out writing assignments. We start on the day the RFP is released because we've only got so much time to put our thoughts together and deliver the proposal that will benefit the government the most. The government may think they're doing us a favor, but in reality, they're making us work at a baseball game on a holiday.

This life isn't perfect—there are moments when you have to choose what's more important to you. Will you work on a holiday? Take a computer with you on vacation? Or do you want to totally unplug to have balance? No response is wrong, it just shows the level of your commitment and drive. At a minimum, you should wear a company logo on a shirt or lanyard. At a maximum, work on holidays every now and then to become a leader in the company and industry.

SWOT ANALYSIS SHEET

STRENGTHS	WEAKNESSES

OPPORTUNITIES	THREATS

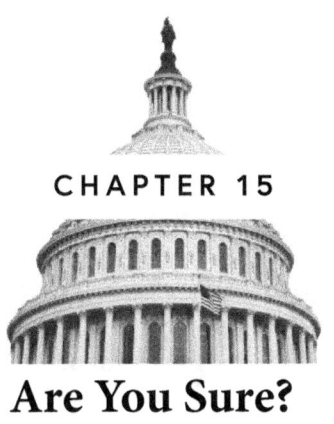

CHAPTER 15

Are You Sure?

"Choices, choices... which way to go?"

—JOHN LOPER [33]

Before we dive into the next section, let's pause for a moment. You've learned how to work for the government, be a good employee, build your brand, communicate well, and be the go-to person for your job… but do you even want to pursue work as a government contractor? There are a lot of drawbacks to government contracting work, but there are benefits, too. Decide for yourself (based on what you've read so far and what I'll say in this chapter) whether it's right for you.

Drawbacks of Working with the Government

Government work is full of bureaucracy (some of us call it bureau*crazy*). In addition, there's no guarantee you won't end up working for a terrible company that takes advantage of you and never gives you a raise. There's also no guarantee you won't end up working for management that doesn't care about you or your ideas (although it would be better than working for a manager who doesn't even know your name).

In contrast, you could apply your skills to "the real world," where you won't have travel restrictions or limiting contractual regulations. You won't even need to get security clearance.

You can find similar work (with equally high pay) by working:

- In sales
- As a CPA
- As a nurse (saving lives)
- At a Fortune 500 company

Why I Love Working with the Government

So why work for the government? Here are the top reasons why I do it:

- I like the flexibility of where I work
- I can work 10 minutes from where I live forever if I want to
- I can navigate the craziness of government bureaucracy and help others do the same
- I work with people who have a drive to make the country better
- I can grow in more directions than I can imagine
- I help those in the military stay safe

Are there elements that suck? Yeah. Some rules are silly, and the equipment we use is typically busted or outdated, but I'd rather do this work than almost anything else—what about you?

Note: *If you want to stop reading the book here, that's fine, but the second half of this book has general leadership advice. Even if you decide government contracting isn't your goal, it could be a helpful read!*

Things to Consider

These are personal traits or behaviors that, while they influence how you fit into a role, can be worked on or refined with time. They don't inherently prevent success, but they might require more investment from you and the organization.

1. Personal Interests and Hobbies:
Your interests outside of work might not directly affect your job performance but can shape how you approach challenges or interact with col-

leagues. For instance, if you are passionate about creative writing, you may bring a different perspective to problem-solving or communication.

2. Confidence:

Confidence can be built. If you lack self-assurance, you may need coaching or exposure to more challenges to build their confidence over time, but it won't completely hinder you in the long run.

3. Work-Life Balance Needs:

Your specific need for work-life balance (e.g., preferring a 9-5 schedule vs. a flexible work arrangement) may need to be aligned with the company's culture, but it's not a dealbreaker if there's flexibility on both sides.

4. Personal Communication Style:

Your natural style of communication (e.g., being more direct vs. more reserved) can be adapted, especially with coaching. Your manager can guide you to effectively communicate in a way that works with their team and the company culture.

(Note: These are all strong areas to mull over about your team members as well, if you choose to become a leader. Feel free to revisit this section to ensure their goals are aligned and you understand their personal styles.)

On Leadership

Before we jump to the next section, let me say this: not all leaders are managers. Not all managers are leaders, either, but all strong, capable employees can be leaders if they choose. People become leaders through experience: by supporting their teammates and being reliable people who support the company and the government. A person's capacity for leadership grows just as they grow over time.

I purposely chose not to call the next section of this book "How to Be a Manager." It's about "How to Be a Leader." You don't have to manage people to be a leader, but becoming a manager means taking on extra responsibilities in terms of contract and employee management. Don't want to be a manager? That's fine, but realize choosing not to be a manager isn't the same as choosing not to be a leader. You may become a leader just by helping those around you.

One More Thing

Not all employees want a leader or manager. Whether they approve of your leadership or not doesn't determine whether you are a leader to some of those around you. You don't choose whom you're a leader to. You can try to reach out as an example to mold them into better employees and people, but at the end of the day, all you can do is get them to show up and (hopefully) do their timecards on time. Manager, leader, and employee relationships are all different, and that's okay.

REMEMBER

Decide for yourself (based on what you've read so far and what I'll say in this chapter) whether it's right for you.

The most important thing for you to remember about working in government support is that effective communication and continuously building your brand (your craft and reputation) are paramount for navigating the complex system. Great communication and a strong brand provide job security amidst contract changes and help foster career growth. Simply knowing the rules is not enough.

NOW ON TO
PART 2

SWOT ANALYSIS SHEET

STRENGTHS	WEAKNESSES

OPPORTUNITIES	THREATS

CHAPTER 16

Foundations of Leadership

"Before you are a leader, success is all about growing yourself. When you become a leader, success is all about growing others."

—ATTRIBUTED TO JACK WELCH [34]

Before you can lead, you should understand your "why." Why do you want to become a leader? Do you want to manage tasks, contracts, or other people? Not everyone cares to be a leader, and not everyone can lead—there's nothing wrong with that. Some people are perfectly happy as contracted employees. This chapter should give you enough information to decide whether leadership is right for you.

Is your goal to make more money as a leader? Let me stop you right there: there's typically not a huge difference between the amount of money a regular employee makes and the amount of money a leader makes, but there's a major increase in responsibility. You'll work more hours and deal with more frustrations as a leader—frustrations including timecards, monthly deliverables, travel requests, and more. You'll be responsible for your work and for the work of everyone under you. You'll be doing two jobs for not much more than the pay of one.

There's a difference between being a good employee and a good leader, so again, ask yourself: Why do you want to be a leader? What's driving you to take on the extra responsibility? Do you want to be important? Do you want to be called "Sir?" Are you doing it because someone else expects you to take the next step up? Do you want to build up your resume and make more money? (Like I said before, making more money might be harder than you realize. It's an achingly long game to make more money in the government.) Or do you want to become a leader because you see the issues around you and you want to fix them? Is it because you want to help other people succeed?

If you haven't thought about your reason yet, think about it now. You need to know your why so it can drive you to succeed, even when your career gets tough. Knowing your reason will help you to do everything you need to do once you reach that position. Some people think there are right and wrong reasons to take action or accept a job offer. Maybe they've got a point, but it's up to you to decide if your reason is the right one for you. The overarching goal should be to create a strong and positive leadership role for yourself, your employees, and your company. If your reason isn't strong enough to get you through the hard times, it'll only be a matter of time before you stop and change your path. Do you have a happy enough memory to anchor you when the storm is raging around you? You are going to need it at some point in your leadership journey.

Action Step

Figure out the reason you want to become a leader. How soon do you plan to step into a leadership role? What will you have to accomplish to get there? On a scale of 1-10, how strong would you say your reason to become a leader is? Do you have more than one reason? What could deter you from pursuing a leadership role, and could it be possible to enjoy those same benefits without the added responsibility of leadership?

An Eye-Opening Leadership Moment

Six months before I got my second task lead position, an employee accidentally sent an email to a personal ".com" account from his ".gov" email account. (He meant to send the email to the other person's ".gov" email account.) You may be thinking, "Who cares?" but in the government, this is a very big deal. There are specific rules about what information can be on what systems, and each employee has to complete training to try to prevent these issues from happening. When the event occurred, the employee followed protocol, taking the exact steps he should have done to minimize the risk caused by the error. The employee notified the (then) task lead, the government contract product manager, and the contract officer. He ensured the email was immediately deleted (from the ".com" inbox, the "deleted" inbox, and from the government email system). He shared the incident with every senior leader he was supposed to share it with.

Eight or nine months after the event (just two or three months into my task lead job), there was a "monthly" IT system investigation [35] report. These reports track security issues, including emails are sent to ".coms," and this incident was on the list. The world ended! The senior leader for the government customer exploded, and since there was nothing else to work on (this is a joke; we were extremely busy), they demanded a full review of the event, including when it happened, why it happened, and what actions were taken after it happened. Thankfully, the employee kept all the records, so the answers to the questions were provided quickly. (Remember the chapter on keeping records? This is why it's important!) There was a paper trail—emails tracking the event with the last task lead and the government.

Unfortunately, this was not the end of it. The government flexed its muscle in typical "If I get called on the carpet, so do you" fashion. The deputy program manager wanted me to punish the employee by putting them on a performance improvement plan and making them retake the training on the proper care of government information and systems. The goal was to make a statement. My response was simple: "I won't do any of that. The employee followed the training by communicating quickly and ensuring the information was handled based on the rules. An error had occurred, but it was identified and handled correctly."

The deputy program manager's reply was less than pleasant: "If you won't do anything, all I can do is take away his system access. Do you want that?"

It sounded like a threat to me, but I replied, "Feel free to do whatever you think is needed. I, however, will not do anything to the employee. Please feel free to call the program manager, and if he, as my boss, directs that we do something to the employee, I will follow those directions." The meeting ended, and I called my contract program manager and told him the entire story so he wouldn't be caught off guard.

The program manager listened and understood my position and my statements to the government, and let me know we wouldn't put the employee on a performance improvement plan, but the training would need to be retaken. I got off the phone and let the employee know what was going on. I also applied for a new job that night—why? This event showed me even if you do everything right (as the employee and previous task lead did), the outcome may not be what should happen, but what one person thinks should happen. At that point in my life, I wasn't mentally prepared to accept that... so I changed my path.

This could be a good place to say, "Know when to leave." The best time to look for a new job is when you have a job. Don't quit as a knee-jerk response—think about it and make a decision. Some people may think, by applying to a new job the same day, I was too reactionary. The truth is I saw the job for what it was and realized I wasn't ready for the position, so I started looking for another one. I don't regret my decision at all—I've had a highly successful career after making that decision, and I'm happy with it.

Know What Leadership Requires of You

When I took on the task lead position, I wasn't fully aware of what leadership would require of me. There are different levels of freedom afforded to each leader, and before you move up, you should be clear on what your duties will be and how they'll be different from the level you're currently at.

For example, during the incident above, I was able to say no as the task lead. However, the contract program manager had to say yes because of the position he was in. Why? Because this is a customer service business, we have to serve the government customers as well as the employees under us. The ".com" email incident taught me I wasn't ready to say yes if I didn't think there was a good reason to do what was asked of me. It took me five more years before I was ready to step into a program manager role.

True leaders don't ask anyone to take an action they wouldn't take themselves. This doesn't mean you need to do everything (or have the background to accomplish everything), but it does mean you need to be fair and honest. It's not about cleaning toilets or working on a Sunday, and actually, both of these tasks might be restricted based on your contract. (This is why, again, you should double-check your contract so you know the rules before you ask for assignments above and beyond a normal day's work.)

When I say to be fair and honest, this is what I mean:
- If you want someone to be a good voice for the company, you should be a better one
- If you want an employee to submit their timecard according to the rules, you'd better be doing it too
- If you want a higher level of responsiveness from an employee, you should be an even more responsive leader to them

"Do as I say, not as I do" has no place in the leadership world. As a leader, you will show who you are and what you believe based on your actions, not based on your words.

SWOT ANALYSIS SHEET

STRENGTHS	WEAKNESSES

OPPORTUNITIES	THREATS

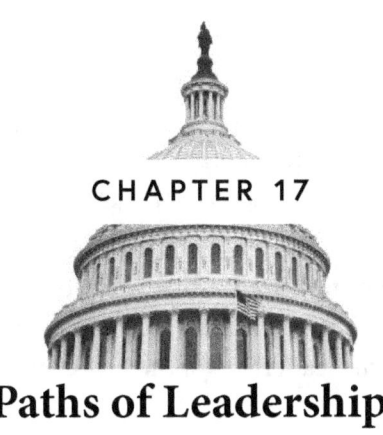

CHAPTER 17

Paths of Leadership

"Management is doing things right; leadership is doing the right things."

— PETER F. DRUCKER, *MANAGEMENT: TASKS, RESPONSIBILITIES, PRACTICES* [36]

You've probably had a mix of leaders: bad leaders (people you report to who you wish you could avoid), and good leaders (people who don't just want you to do your job and have the right tools, but who care about you as a person). This chapter highlights both good and bad leaders, as well as the impact each type of leader can have. The truth is no matter how hard a team tries to tune it out, a bad leader can negatively impact a team. Conversely, a great leader can have a positive impact, bringing even an average team to greatness.

A Bad Manager

One of the worst experiences I ever had with upper management came down to two major flaws: a bad attitude and a lack of experience. This manager was in charge of the whole group but had never worked in this specific career field before. You may be thinking, "Inexperience in a specific career field isn't always a problem." You're right—in many fields, a good leader can come in with little to no experience, and as long as they're willing to learn and have general knowledge, they can still be successful. However, this was not one of those career fields. This was a field requiring years (arguably decades) of work to understand the rules, nuance, and unusual moments within it.

Great leaders in this field know more than the field itself—they navigate the field while still providing leadership, mentorship, and career growth opportunities for the employees under them. To be the ultimate person in charge of this career field, leaders need to understand everything we talked about in part one of this book. They need to know the rules, the craft, and the system. They have to be able to communicate all of it down to the workforce and up to the leadership of the bigger agency.

This person didn't have a full understanding of what it meant to lead people who wrote government contracts, and was not able to understand why tasks took the amount of time they did, or why we had to create the documents we created. He also couldn't understand why certain rules existed to protect the general public, the companies wanting to work with the government, and the employees who were writing the contracts.

This manager wasn't only unqualified, which would have been bad enough in this field, but he saw the field as an obstruction to progress. He thought the work being done was nothing more than an administrative burden—one slowing down the progress of the people who mattered and made it harder for them to get the tools and knowledge they needed to succeed. He did not care about federal laws in place to ensure we wrote fair and honest contracts attracting high-quality, qualified people. He didn't care that the law required him to put the right items and information into the hands of those "doing the real work."

He was not only unaware of the laws. He also did not value them and would go over the workforce and sign contracts without following all the required steps to award those contracts. Needless to say, this manager created a huge issue with employees who'd been at the office for decades and were now more knowledgeable than their boss.

This is especially scary considering what would happen later. Many employees weren't prepared to defend the positions placed in front of them. This specific location had previously failed at training many of the employees about following the rules, the processes created because of those rules, and how to defend decisions made by following the rules and processes in order to be awarded contracts. In other words, several employees from that office had to find new jobs very quickly, and did… yet they still knew more about the requirements than their leader.

Consequences of Bad "Leadership"

Bad leaders create a ripple effect, poisoning the entire office. Here are a few of the negative consequences of bad leadership:

- Rumors/gossip
- A toxic workplace
- Tension/stress in the office
- Stagnation instead of growth
- Disengagement from the work(which kills quality)
- Turnover, which results in having to train new employees (which results in lower work completion rates)
- Creation of a "yes man" culture
- More resignations

A Great Leader

One of my previous managers was exceptional. Over time, he proved to be more than a good leader—he proved to be an adept mentor who supported me even after he was not my direct boss anymore. He has since passed away, but in the decade he went from being my boss to my call-back support person, he helped me grow as a person, provided career growth opportunities, and taught me how to become a leader. In my youth, I was rough around the edges (I'm putting it lightly), but he took me under his wing and helped me see the bigger picture. He showed me yes, sometimes life is hard and it sucks, but you have to keep growing to figure out how to get past the problems.

"Embrace the suck," he'd say. I heard it a lot from him, but the first time he ever said it to me, I was sitting in his office to talk about what was happening at the government site. We reviewed my work, who I was supporting, and how much travel was needed to do the work. At the time, I didn't realize he was looking at our conversation from two different perspectives. On one level, he cared about what I was doing and was equipping me to do my job. On the other level, he was getting the information he needed as a program manager by making sure I was busy enough and I was doing work that followed the contract requirements. He was also seeing if he'd need to request more travel money for the contract and taking care of other details only a PM would know.

"It sucks I don't have a desk yet," I said. "I've been working here for about a month, and I'm still working out of 'hot desks.' I need to find a new one every day just to do my work!" (A "hot desk" is a temporary desk set up for people who are traveling, so they can have a place to work. The first person who finds an open "hot desk" gets to work at it—I didn't have a predictable place to work during that time and couldn't store anything there. The reason I had to use them for so long was there were too many employees at the site for everyone to have a desk. I wasn't the only person who didn't have a desk, but I was annoyed by it, and I'd never been without my own desk before.)

"Embrace the suck," he said. "Sure, not having a desk sucks in some ways, but it's great in others. Most people are lazy—they're not going to go out of their way to find which desk you're at. They'll just send you an email about whatever they need. Tell me: how many times do you get interrupted at work because someone comes to your desk?"

I had to admit, "Never." I got what he was saying at a high level at the time, but I still wanted a desk. It took me years to realize the greatest rewards in life sometimes come through struggle, frustration, annoyance, and learning to embrace the suck. Now I know that almost everything has a positive and a negative to it. Things that suck can give you freedom, future opportunities, or a buffer from people who don't want to embrace the suck. The more you embrace it, learn it, and keep it close to you, the less things will suck in the future. You'll handle those circumstances with minimal stress and worry because you've dealt with them before, and even if they're new (you will always find new things that suck), you'll have a history of "embracing the suck" to help you adapt and get through the circumstances.

Consequences of Great Leadership

In the same way there are negative consequences for bad leadership, there are great results for good leadership. Here are some of them:

- You'll be more resilient during challenges (you'll handle problems/disappointment better)
- You'll have the confidence to do your job without looking over your shoulder
- You'll be better equipped to become a leader
- You'll have no power struggles

Great leadership has a positive overflow effect:

Input (Starting point)	Output (What it leads to)
Employees are comfortable enough to ask questions	Employees have more understanding
Employees have more understanding	Employees do faster work
Employees do faster work	Employees have more total work completed
Employees have more total work completed	Better company morale
Better company morale	Better employee retention
Better employee retention	Higher levels of knowledge and more comfort within the team

SWOT ANALYSIS SHEET

STRENGTHS	WEAKNESSES

OPPORTUNITIES	THREATS

CHAPTER 18

Employee Support

"To manage, one must lead. To lead, one must understand the work that he and his people are responsible for."

— W. EDWARDS DEMING, OUT OF THE CRISIS [37]

Employees need to be supported and equipped to do their jobs. They need tools, knowledge, training, etc., and they shouldn't feel overly burdened or impeded in their abilities to provide high levels of support. When appropriate, leaders protect their employees from the government. Employees are our greatest resource—they're the company's biggest asset and the "face of the company" to the customers. While that's true, one assumption leaders can get wrong is automatically assuming high-performing employees should be put into leadership positions. This may not be a wise idea, and I'll explain why it should be looked at on a deeper level in this chapter and the following one.

Our Jobs as Government Contracting Leaders

There are three facets of success for government contract leaders. A good leader in this field must provide success for:

- the company
- the employee
- the customer

Within each of these three spheres, a leader should provide as much knowledge, support (tools and other resources), and communication as possible. Since every relationship is different, communication is different within each sphere as well. That's why I've set aside different chapters for communication as employees and leaders, and why leadership communication is broken down even further. Since each person communicates differently, it's important to be aware of how everyone engages in order to ensure communication is clearly understood.

The tricky part about these three facets or spheres of success is it's nearly impossible to keep all three happy all of the time. Each facet has its own concerns, values, and priorities, and you're the "middleman" in it all.

For example, employees would be overjoyed if each one of them were given a raise. (For the sake of hyperbole, let's say we give each employee a million dollars a year.) The employees would be thrilled, but there would be major contract and government failures if we were to implement the raise. On the other hand, getting employees to work for free (again, for the sake of hyperbole) would make the company and the government customer over-joyed for a while, but employees would be miserable and they'd quit in search of better work. Even promoting a high-performing employee who does a great job of supporting the customer can come with risks, because when you add the responsibility of supporting other employees on top of their current responsibilities, they may struggle. In that case, promoting a high performer may not be successful for anyone: employee, customer, or company. (So, how do you know whom to promote? Learn more about employee placement in the next chapter.)

Key Values of the Three Spheres and How Managers Balance Them

1. Employee
Employees are focused on their personal growth, job satisfaction, and their overall work-life balance. Their priorities often revolve around:
- **Fair Compensation**: Competitive salary, benefits, and perfor-mance-based rewards.
- **Work-Life Balance**: Flexible working hours, remote work options, and reasonable workloads to maintain personal and family com-mitments.

- **Job Security**: A sense of stability in their position and long-term employment prospects.
- **Career Development**: Opportunities for skill development, promotions, and career growth within the organization.
- **Work Environment**: A supportive, inclusive, and positive work culture, good relationships with colleagues, and a healthy work atmosphere.
- **Recognition and Appreciation**: Being valued and acknowledged for hard work, efforts, and contributions.
- **Autonomy and Empowerment**: Having some degree of control over how they do their work, along with the ability to make decisions.
- **Purpose and Meaning**: Feeling their work contributes to a greater purpose or has personal significance.

2. Company

The company, as an entity, is driven by long-term success, profitability, and growth. Its priorities include:

- **Profitability**: Maximizing revenue, controlling costs, and achieving financial success.
- **Growth and Expansion**: Scaling operations, entering new markets, and growing the business over time.
- **Sustainability**: Maintaining operational stability, minimizing risk, and ensuring the business can continue in the long term.
- **Innovation**: Staying competitive by introducing new products, services, or improvements.
- **Brand Reputation**: Building a strong, positive reputation in the market, attracting customers, partners, and talent.
- **Employee Productivity**: Ensuring employees are performing efficiently and are motivated to achieve company and customer goals.
- **Compliance and Legal Considerations**: Adhering to regulations, laws, and industry standards.
- **Stakeholder Value**: Delivering value to shareholders, investors, and other key stakeholders.

3. Government Customer

The government's goals are simple: to get what it wants, when it wants it, for what it thinks it should cost. Its focus includes:

- **Cost:** Meeting the contractual cost constraints while accomplishing the schedule and performance needs of the contract.
- **Schedule:** Fulfilling all performance requirements within cost constraints to ensure the ability to engage on "follow-on contract" needs linked to the schedule.
- **Performance:** Ensuring all objectives of the requirement are met to fulfill the contractual requirements.

Manager Responsibilities and Needs

Managers have broad responsibilities—their jobs are to balance the needs of their teams, the government customers, and the companies. Their priorities tend to focus on:

- **Team Performance**: Ensuring the team meets goals, deadlines, and requirements.
- **Employee Development**: Supporting the growth and development of team members, offering coaching, mentoring, and training.
- **Resource Management**: Allocating resources effectively (time, personnel, budget) to meet objectives and achieve goals.
- **Communication**: Maintaining clear and open lines of communication between team members, upper management, and other departments.
- **Achieving Organizational Goals**: Aligning team objectives with company-wide goals, ensuring the team contributes effectively to the company's success.
- **Problem-Solving and Conflict Resolution**: Addressing challenges, resolving conflicts, and removing obstacles potentially hindering team productivity.
- **Performance Reviews and Accountability**: Conducting evaluations, providing feedback, and holding team members accountable for their work.

Key Differences:
- **Employees** are primarily concerned with their personal well-being, career growth, and the day-to-day work environment.
- **The company** is driven by long-term strategic goals, profitability, growth, and sustainability, with an eye on how everything aligns to ensure overall success.
- **The government** is driven by a combination of short and long-term goals linking to specific requirements placed on a contract.
- **Managers** must balance their team's needs with the company's goals, ensuring high performance while managing resources effectively.

Common Ground:

While there are distinct differences in priorities, there is often some overlap. For example, managers and employees both value a positive work culture and professional development. Similarly, both employees and companies care about achieving organizational goals, though they may see success from different angles.

Finding a balance between these interests is key to creating a productive, healthy work environment that aligns the motivations of employees, customers, managers, and the company as a whole.

Building Trust with New Employees

Your team will consist of some employees who are more experienced in their work environment and some who are new to it. Remember, some new employees are coming from toxic and unhelpful workplaces where they were told to just figure it out or were demeaned if they asked any questions. For at least the first three months on the job, an employee is "feeling it out" and determining whether it's even safe to talk to their boss about their real questions or concerns.

During this time, it's critical not just to have an "open-door" policy, but to check in on a regular basis to see if they need help with anything. If they never take you up on your offer to help, you've already learned about their communication style—they prefer to keep their head down at work and get tasks done rather than engage, and they probably thrive on solo work. If they do take you up on it, they'll do so knowing you've offered to help more than they've asked, and they'll feel more comfortable asking for clarity in the future.

Everything they need help with will give you more information—their concerns, their questions, and how those questions are worded. How they choose to communicate with you (whether verbally, written, etc.) will create a pattern showing you their styles, personalities, goals, and priorities. Based on how they find solutions or what they gravitate toward, you'll learn how they collaborate with you and the rest of the team. You'll learn who's detail-oriented and technical (ie: the best types for head-down, precise work that can be done solo) and who's social and outgoing (ie: the best types to send to a convention or other event where the goal is to generate interest in the company or product).

If you've just become a leader, remember it'll take some time for the experienced employees to get to know you in this role, too. They may have worked alongside you as coworkers, but they haven't experienced your leadership yet, and they don't know what to expect from the shift. Give them time to learn your leadership style.

Action Item

Add weekly or bi-weekly check-ins to your schedule so they won't slip off your radar. Create a spreadsheet so you can track any needs or concerns coming up and how you're dealing with them. What's your action plan to tackle the concern? Who do you need to follow up with? Be sure to revisit the spreadsheet before the next meeting or check in with the employee to ensure they are updated on the progress.

When Employees Leave

It will be hard when employees leave, especially if you've taken the time to grow them and help them become better professionals. Try not to take it personally, though. People leave for all kinds of reasons, and while some of those reasons can be fixed or managed to keep employees on, sometimes you'll be "handcuffed" and unable to stop the situation from happening. Learn which situations are which (fixable vs. unfixable) and support the employees through them.

Fortunately, some employees leave and then come back. These "boomerangs" leave to gain more knowledge, experience, money, etc., then return to the company. A boomerang employee is great. Sometimes they come back because they learned what they were chasing wasn't what they thought it was. They may not want the same lifestyle or responsibility anymore. Sometimes they learn the grass isn't greener on the other side of the fence (even if they get plenty of "green" in compensation). Other times, they find success, and you're able to provide the next step up in their career. If they view you highly enough to want to work together again, that's a win for everyone.

Never say never—as long as you're doing everything in your power to give employees the strongest experience in a company, you have the potential to create boomerang employees.

Action Item

Create a spreadsheet with general information about your employees. (This should be different from the weekly check-in spreadsheet you're creating above.) What situations and environments do they thrive in? What areas are difficult for them? Where do you think they can grow, and what are their goals? Add as much information as you can. Continue to use this spreadsheet regularly (and when you check in with them, if needed) to ensure you've got a bird's eye view of the unique attributes of your employees.

Here are some ideas on what to include on the spreadsheet:

- Goals
- Birthdate
- Personality
- Work anniversary
- Family info/priorities
- Work style (social, focused, etc.)
- Best environments for the employee to work in
- Dealbreakers (employee doesn't want to travel, etc.)
- Important career conversations you've had with the employee

REMEMBER

If you've just become a leader, remember it'll take some time for the experienced employees to get to know you in this role, too.

SWOT ANALYSIS SHEET

STRENGTHS	WEAKNESSES

OPPORTUNITIES	THREATS

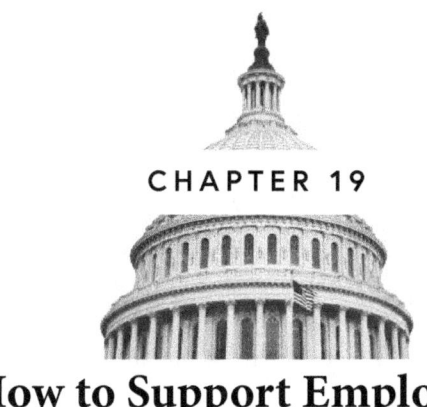

CHAPTER 19

How to Support Employees

"You get the best out of others when you give the best of yourself."

—ATTRIBUTED TO HARVEY S. FIRESTONE [38]

To support employees, you need to be willing to have hard conversations about the employee's capabilities, plans for growth, and limits to success. A limit to success can come in the form of less education, less experience, lower interpersonal skills, etc., than another role requires. These obstacles are not long-term dealbreakers—you should always encourage growth— but they might prevent your employee from getting the next promotion.

Employee support comes down to communication (more about that in the next chapter). For now, though, you'll need to know the basics about how to assess and support your employees. You'll have to be open, honest, and willing to communicate the results of your assessment, despite the fact your employees may not take it well or may choose to look elsewhere for work because they didn't like your answers. No matter what questions or concerns the employees have, be willing to answer their questions. Provide "the why" behind your reasons—doing this helps them feel heard, valued, and understood.

Employee Placement

To help employees advance, you've got to see them as they are, not as you want them to be. You've got to know what they want, what skills they have, how they perform, and how they interact with their coworkers.

Finding a good fit for employees may sound straightforward, but it's more than matching skills and capabilities—it's also about personality alignment and more. If you put a wonderful employee with a strong skill set but poor interpersonal skills into an office where water cooler talk is preferred over actual work, you'll set them up for disappointment and failure. Any employee who's got great abilities in one sense and weaker abilities in another shouldn't be moved to a place where their weaknesses will be highlighted unless you are ready and able to provide the support and aid they need to shore up those areas of weakness. Supporting an employee is much more than an open-door policy—it's getting them the education they need, and giving them the time they need in the job so they can qualify for the next position they want to advance to.

The factors you'll need to weigh to find the right position for an employee include:

- Job specifics
- Office dynamics
- Personality differences
- Wants for today and tomorrow
- And more

It can be hard to balance the fact here are different levels of jobs and different levels of performers. To drive this point home, let me give you a few more examples of bad fits. You may think it's harmless to put a high-performing employee in a low-engagement position, but the employee would quickly get bored, lose interest, and start looking for another challenge. It's not good to put a low-performing employee in a high-engagement position, either—they'll get overwhelmed and fail to provide the needed support. What it comes down to is putting each of your people in positions to succeed. (Take a look at "Checking Employee Fit for a New Position" in the back of this book for more information.)

Here's a recap of what factors to look at when addressing employee fit:

- **Education and Experience:** These get employees in the door for an interview, but should also be on your mind if you think an employee may fit a better position now or in the future based on their background.

- **Interpersonal skills/office dynamics:** This is vital for team integration. The right person on the wrong team will fail.

- **Engagement level/performance:** Again, employees should be put in environments where they'll match with the team's energy, whether high or low engagement.

- **Overall goals:** This may not be immediately usable information (like education and experience, for example) but should be kept at the forefront of your mind in case new positions or opportunities for growth come up for the employee.

- **Hard and soft skills:** Hard skills (proficiency with Teams, SharePoint, GFEBS) and soft skills (adaptability, attention to detail, communication) should be relevant to what the role requires or is best suited for.

- **Overall understanding:** This is a sum of all the aforementioned parts and a plan for the future. Sometimes the employee will remain in the same position until their time with the company is completed. Other times, you will be able to create a path for them to take and find opportunities for them to grow. Sometimes, you will need to wait and see how things pan out a year from now.

Matching the right person to the right position is often better than matching a person to the right company or matching them to a position for future growth. Many times, I've put people into positions because they fit there at the time. I thought this was a short-term solution and expected them to grow into new abilities and responsibilities, but those plans failed to materialize. Sometimes it was a pacing issue: I tried to grow the employee too fast or too slow. Sometimes it was because a life change impacted their wants and outlooks on their careers. Sometimes plans simply changed, and we adapted to those changes. As leaders, we do the best we can to fit people into positions and help them grow the best possible talents at the right times so the employees can grow alongside the company.

Action Step

Using the spreadsheet you created at the end of the last chapter, determine whether your employees seem to want to advance to other work or are comfortable in their current positions. What is needed for the employees who would like to advance? Which jobs would they be suited to? Sketch out a plan to make it happen and discuss it with your employees.

Bonus: Find out if any of your employees are experiencing burnout—there's a helpful resource on how to deal with that at the back of the book!

Helping Good Employees Become Great Employees

Before you can help good employees become great employees, you've got to know what the difference is between the two. A good employee learns the rules and the craft. A great employee learns the rules and craft, then adds overall understanding to the role. A leader's job is to help employees gain understanding so they can become great. The most amazing, trusted contractors deepen their comprehension of each of their tasks and know how to keep the government out of trouble. As a leader, one of your tasks will be to know the difference between a good employee and one who can become a great employee (even if they choose not to take on a leadership role).

Employee Recognition

Recognition is key in helping an employee feel like they're part of a team that values and cares about them. There are different types of recognition, but the primary ones used within a government contracting context are monetary recognition and words of encouragement or gratitude. Monetary recognition comes in the form of bonuses, raises, or spot awards. Encouraging words can come in the form of an email on a random Tuesday, thanking an employee for their valuable contributions, or can show up as employee spotlights in a quarterly company newsletter.

Building employee morale and corporate connection can be a challenge as a leader. Most employees in customer support aren't all in the same location, but instead are on-site with the government customer. You've heard the old phrase, "Out of sight, out of mind," right? It's even worse when you're in a different location. When it comes to employee recognition, a better saying is "Out of *site*, out of mind," which is why leaders in government contracting need to be intentional. If you're not actively engaged in staying connected, you can lose what makes the company great to work for and what makes you a great person to work with. Bottom line: to become a leader who people remember in a positive light, learn how to give recognition and help your company engage with employees.

Quarterly Newsletters

One final note for this chapter: Quarterly newsletters can be a great way to provide employee recognition. They may seem cheesy, but they show what the company is, who they work for, what the leadership team values, and that the company cares enough about its employees to keep them in the loop. When people feel valued, heard, seen, and encouraged, they're happier in their work and their lives. People want a sense of ownership and accomplishment for what they do, and even if you don't see your employees every day, you can let them know you appreciate them. Newsletters also enable you to show your sense of ownership in the company and lead by example!

If you're not sure what to include in a newsletter, here are some ideas:

- A review of your company's core values
- A section for employee achievements and awards
- A review of policies, procedures, and regulations to follow
- Reminders about health benefits, offers, and incentives for employees
- A review of charitable donations or causes the company has invested in
- A review of the previous quarter, including special company events (with photos)
- A look ahead at the goals for the next quarter and a plan on how to achieve them
- A space for employees to celebrate family milestones (this fosters work-life balance)

REMEMBER

When it comes to employee recognition, a better saying is 'Out of site, out of mind,' which is why leaders in government contracting need to be intentional.

SWOT ANALYSIS SHEET

STRENGTHS	WEAKNESSES

OPPORTUNITIES	THREATS

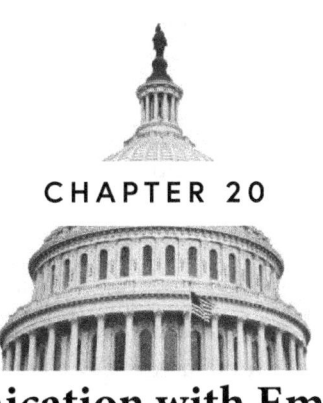

CHAPTER 20

Communication with Employees

"The great enemy of communication... is the illusion of it."

—WILLIAM H. WHYTE, FORTUNE MAGAZINE [39]

Picture this: you've given an employee a task to do, and they've agreed to do it. Now you can relax and pat yourself on the back for a job well done, right? Wrong! Agreement is not the same as understanding, and failing to realize this can cost you and your company. This is one of the reasons why leaders are so quick to create templates and checklists for employees to use. Even then, though, things can go wrong, especially if templates and checklists haven't been updated or the protocol has changed.

The Burden of Required Speed

During the pandemic (and for several years afterward), there was a shift from on-site work to remote work. Since I'm now back in the corporate office, I've seen how people I've covered aren't able to keep up with all their tasks. Program managers should always strive to provide timely responses and stay in front of the wave of information.

Providing quick, thoughtful responses can have the following positive effects on your work as a leader:

- **Better professional relationships.** Prompt responses prove you value the people you're working with and want to help them.

- **Greater efficiency.** While it may be tempting to hold off on sending an emai responsel, waiting too long could cause you to forget important details.
- **Better decisions.** Because all the details will be fresh in your mind, chances are you'll make better decisions.
- **Less anxiety.** Putting tasks off can add to the mental load you carry, which contributes to anxiety.

Note: if you are feeling frustrated as a result of an email you've gotten, it's okay to buy yourself enough time to formulate a response by politely saying, "Thank you for bringing this to my attention. I am considering the situation now and plan to give you my answer in [period of time]." This way, the person knows they've been heard and you're not ignoring them, but it gives you time to cool off, draft a few responses, talk it over with someone, or get an extra pair of eyes on the response you plan to send.

Words Matter

When you give someone a task, what you expect is probably going to be very different from what the other person hears or how they understand it. (Remember the image from chapter eight? It's a combination of what you said and what they heard.) Different people engage differently—whether it's due to the environment they were raised in, how they communicate, or what kind of day they've had. Make sure you and the employee are on the same page and welcome discussion and questions about the task if they get stuck at any point during the task's execution.

Creating Complex Instructions

If you've got to give complex instructions to an employee, there's a fine line you need to walk. Instructions should be detailed enough for the employee to follow them well and without any issues, but on the other hand, they shouldn't be overly detailed to the point of confusion. I'll give some examples of each part of this equation.

First, provide detailed instructions. If you're asking a team member to create a month-end brief on the current contract status and expected need dates for additional funds (including risks and upcoming tasks potentially impacting the cost and schedule), you would need to provide in-depth information. You'll likely use templates, ask to see their drafts, facilitate Q&A sessions, talk about and document changes over time, and provide clarification when the brief isn't presented in the desired way.

The way you choose to provide information to the employee (and how you interact with them) will also depend on the timing: if you're introducing a plan like this, can you expect the first month-end meeting to be perfect? Or will you allow the first few months to be a learning period, with the expectation that by month three, the employee will nail it? Neither outcome is right or wrong, but the level of communication and instruction should coincide with the expectations and the amount of time you're willing to spend on these tasks. (Perfect month-end briefs don't just happen—they are the result of hard work from the employee and the manager.)

The flipside of providing detailed instructions is to add enough flexibility for the employee to use their discretion. Being overly specific can sometimes be a downfall. For example, if you tell an employee to include specific people in an email, they may misunderstand and think you want them to include only the people on your list. Doing so could create problems: certain people who should be notified via email may be missed if the employee takes you too literally. There's a quick fix to this, though: instead of saying, "Include these people in the email," you can say, "Include these people in the email, along with anyone else who would need this information."

Getting Feedback

As a leader, you should welcome feedback from your employees. This may not make sense to you, but bear with me—it's not a sign of weakness to ask for feedback. It doesn't mean you're lacking in confidence or ability. To the contrary, you ask for feedback so you can become a better leader, stronger communicator, and more capable teacher. You do it so you can see the road ahead and smoothly navigate yourself and your team around the obstacles. No one is perfect, and open conversations help employees feel comfortable with the leadership you provide. Employees will only voice their opinions on how you support, engage, and help them when they're comfortable. Asking for feedback shows you're willing to grow and improve as a leader, and getting feedback will grant valuable insights into what you do well and what you may do poorly. You want your employees to continue growing and learning, and asking for feedback is a way for you to show those same qualities of continual growth.

Asking for feedback isn't the same as promising to implement feedback. As a leader, you don't need to (and you honestly shouldn't) implement every piece of feedback you get. Not all the feedback you get will be valid. Everyone's got an opinion, and most of those opinions are formed with a limited view of the battlefield, so assess the value of the feedback before you decide what to implement. You also don't need to request feedback from every employee, but you should always be open to feedback. As you talk with multiple people, you'll analyze the feedback and start to see trends. Those trends will be more helpful than one-off comments because they'll show you the bigger picture.

Prepare to Fail

You'll fail at communication over and over. You'll be shocked at how some people understand a statement versus what you really mean when you say something. You'll have to modify your statements several times to ensure you're being clear and communicating what you want to say. Keep at it— communication is as important as it is difficult, and you will continue to grow if you expect to fail and make allowance for it instead of being disappointed and frustrated every time a conversation or task doesn't go the way you thought it would.

Action Step

Create a folder for feedback. This feedback should include anything pertaining to you, your team, or your work. Ensure you've got one folder for positive feedback and one for negative feedback. Be sure to follow up on the negative feedback and take steps to correct any valid concern or criticism.

REMEMBER

Agreement is not the same as understanding, and failing to realize this can cost you and your company.

SWOT ANALYSIS SHEET

STRENGTHS	WEAKNESSES

OPPORTUNITIES	THREATS

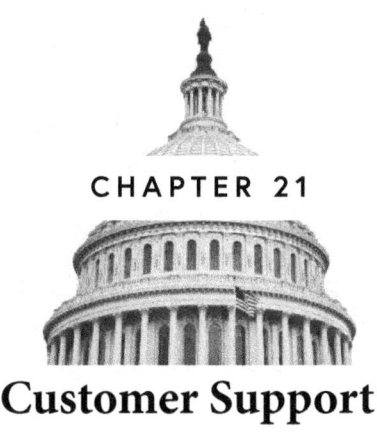

CHAPTER 21

Customer Support

"A leader takes people where they want to go. A great leader takes people where they don't necessarily want to go, but ought to be."

—ATTRIBUTED TO ROSALYNN CARTER [40]

You are in the customer service business, and your job is to be as knowledgeable as possible. However, unlike "the real world," the government knows how the sausage gets made because they're alongside you, in the same office, watching it happen. You provide support, insight, and guidance to the customer. As a leader, you don't have to be the smartest person in the room when it comes to every topic, but you have to know what the employees are doing so you can provide the correct support to the government. One of the main goals is to ensure you have the right people in the right places to provide the right support.

Another component of becoming knowledgeable includes gathering knowledge about the customer itself. Learn about how the government feels about your employees. Understand their viewpoint on the rules and requirements they must follow, and find out what gaps they have. Learn about anything the customer is willing to share so you can manage their expectations.

If you're a subcontractor, you'll have to craft these conversations carefully since you're in a tricky position. You don't want to put yourself, the customer, or the prime contractor in a negative position. There are many rules governing how conversations can be conducted, and the prime contract holder and the government customer must communicate properly with one another.

Challenges in Providing Support to the Government

There are two main roadblocks to your ability to provide support to the government. Each one has its own solutions, but the second roadblock is far more complex than the first.

Challenge #1:
The Government Customer Doesn't Know What They Want

If this is the case, you could be sitting around for days on end, waiting to receive instructions. To help the customer (and give yourself something to do), you've got to be proactive. Look for gaps in processes and help the government see and understand those gaps, too. Provide suggestions on how to improve your processes.

Challenge #2:
The Government Has Unrealistic Requirements and Expectations

Sometimes, the government's expectations are off. They may want something in 10 days that would take a strong, capable, and knowledgeable employee 30 days to do. It's our job to provide what they're asking for, but we should also remind them of the fast/cheap/right rule.

If you haven't heard of the fast/cheap/right rule yet, here's how it works: you only get two. If you want it fast and right, it won't be cheap. You'll need to increase your resources to meet the goal. If you want it cheap and fast, it won't be right. You'll have to cut corners or make assumptions to get the end product quickly. If you want it cheap and right, it won't be fast. You'll need to give it more time. In some cases, taking extra time costs more money, but in other cases, taking more time saves money. It'll be up to you to provide all the possible benefits and drawbacks of each course the government is considering.

Give Them What They Want (But Not Always How They Asked for It)

Think of projects in the sense of their full life cycles. This encompasses not just what each item you build does but also how to build and maintain the item, too. Starting with the ending in mind may lead you to design the end item differently to account for the broader life cycle. Customer support means giving the government customer what they want, even if it's not necessarily how they asked for it.

This includes managing the customer's expectations, which is a difficult skill but a necessary one.

Some of the things the government wants are part of the normal cycle of business, like wanting to meet a person before they're hired. This enables the government and the potential employee to have conversations about the office, the position, the expectations, and the normal tasks that will occur. It gives each party (customer and potential hire) the ability to see what it's going to be like if the person is hired. The candidate may decide not to go forward after such a meeting. They get a vote, of course, and it's up to them to decide whether they'd like to continue.

Other requests the government makes are unacceptable. One example of this is some government offices ask candidates to complete a practical "project" before they're hired. They require candidates to do work for free that the government can use in the future, whether or not the candidate is hired. This practice has become normal in some US job markets, but it takes unfair advantage of a candidate and violates the labor category requirements the government is held to.

The truth is, the government doesn't actually have any input into who the company hires. It's the company's job to provide individuals who meet the requirements for a position on contract.

The contractor has the right to:
- Choose whether or not to facilitate a meet and greet
- Choose whether or not to present a resume for review

- Choose how to fill the position—whether they want to involve the government or just let them know the position has been filled, when the person is starting, and the person they've hired meets all the role's requirements

These conversations should be carefully handled by the contract company's leadership to balance providing quality personnel without increasing the amount of time and overall burden of providing personnel. Leaders should strive to hold these conversations in a way that avoids creating a negative relationship with the government since they prefer not to be told "no."

As I said earlier, providing support to the government can be tricky. How you'll communicate depends on several factors:
- Whether it's an end item or services contract
- Whether you're a prime or subcontractor
- Whether it's a cost/time/material or fixed-price contract
- How much the contract is worth/how much the contract value is, etc.

A Word of Advice to Leaders in Subcontract Roles

Remember, if you're a leader in a subcontract role, your customer is the government, but the prime contractor comes first. This means the prime should be the only one talking to the government about:
- The contract
- Employee performance
- New positions needed for the contract

This is unique to government support: only there do you have employees who interact with the government every day, but who are generally not allowed to do the above tasks. As a subcontractor, you've got to learn how to navigate situations where the government wants to speak directly to you because you're familiar with them and work with them all the time. Some-times, the government manager isn't aware of the rules they have to follow. It may seem unimportant to redirect the government manager to the prime, but it's very serious. I have seen companies overstep their privity of contract rules, and the prime kicked them off the contract for it. The company destroyed its relationship with the prime contractor and with the government in that office.

Correct communication in line with rules and regulations is a must because:

- No one likes feeling like someone went around them
- No one likes feeling like they were left out of conversations and decisions
- No one likes being told the sub is going to get work, and the prime is going to have to deal with it

Do all you can to be open, and don't step on your dance partner's toes!

REMEMBER

In government support, especially as a subcontractor, strictly adhere to communication protocols to avoid severe consequences like contract termination and damaged relationships.

SWOT ANALYSIS SHEET

STRENGTHS	WEAKNESSES

OPPORTUNITIES	THREATS

CHAPTER 22

Communication with the Customer

"The most important thing in communication is to hear what isn't being said."

—PETER DRUCKER, 1989 INTERVIEW WITH BILL MOYERS[41]

Your main duty in a customer support capacity with the government is to ensure the customer is happy. When the customer is happy, they are more likely to cooperate, support your efforts, and ultimately become an advocate for you. Satisfaction in government work is not just about delivering results—it's about creating a positive experience for the customer in every interaction.

It's a balancing act. In the government support world, you must balance accuracy, efficiency, and friendliness. These three elements combine to make bureaucratic processes feel smoother for the customer. Government-related tasks sometimes feel impersonal, rigid, or frustrating due to bureaucracy and regulations, even for the government customer. Make the customer feel that their needs are understood. Address their needs personally and promptly. Creating rapport can change the tone of interactions and make you and the customer feel like partners working toward a shared goal.

Happy customers will view you positively, provide helpful feedback, and continue to engage with you—this will enable you to succeed in your role. Happy customers are repeat customers, which translates to continued funding, additional contracts, and ongoing positive outcomes.

Effective Communication: The Art of Professionalism and Empathy

Professionalism isn't just being formal—it's also being emotionally intelligent. Emotional intelligence is empathy, which is the ability to understand the emotions and reactions of the customer and respond with care. Many customers in government settings are under immense pressure due to limited resources, complex regulations, and public scrutiny. This stress evolves into frustration, making communication more challenging.

When a project is delayed, customers can easily become defensive or upset. As a government support professional, your job is to explain the situation, actively listen to their concerns, and respond in a way that reduces tension. People want to feel heard, understood, and respected. It is your responsibility to be the bearer of good and bad news and help the government navigate all of it.

Being emotionally intelligent means knowing when to escalate an issue, offer solutions, or offer a listening ear. The key is to balance professionalism with emotional sensitivity. When customers know you understand their pain points, they're far more likely to work with you to find solutions.

Develop the skill of being direct but tactful. Customers want clarity and honesty—a straightforward conversation that's not harsh. For example, if there's a delay in processing a contract due to an unexpected review period, you could say:

"I understand it's frustrating to have delays, and I empathize with the urgency. Unfortunately, due to an extended review period mandated by our internal processes, the timeline needs to shift by a week. However, I'll make sure we can get everything moving as smoothly as possible from now on. Let me know if you'd like to discuss any immediate steps we can take to ensure the next phases stay on track."

This conversation shows professionalism by acknowledging the issue, offering transparency, and creating a partnership with the customer. Being open and honest shows the places with bottlenecks and enables the customer to engage and raise flags to the issues causing delays.

Handling Difficult News: Honesty Without Alienation

Bring bad news quickly—customers appreciate transparency and quick action when problems arise. "Bad news does not get better with time," [42] and delaying a difficult conversation often only makes it worse. (Remember why I decided to write this book in the first place?) Don't avoid sharing bad news to soften the blow or minimize the impact. Instead, acknowledge the issue head-on and offer a potential solution or way forward.

For example, if a funding issue might delay a project, don't just tell the customer the funds have been cut. Instead, present the facts while inviting collaboration:

"Funding for this project has been reduced due to new budget constraints based on a mark from the hill. However, I've already looked into alternative funding options across the program, and I'm in touch with other departments to ensure we can meet the most critical needs within the revised budget. I'll keep you informed. Let's discuss how we can best prioritize the remaining tasks and update the contracts as needed."

Presenting both the problem and the solution shifts the conversation from frustration to problem-solving. This constructive approach helps the customer feel involved, keeping them engaged in finding a solution rather than being a passive recipient of bad news.

No matter what, be responsive. Don't let emails sit in your inbox. Don't let phone messages or texts go unanswered. You don't have to have the complete answer right away—just don't be silent. Good customer service means keeping the customer informed at every step!

The Importance of Offering Solutions: Creating Options for the Customer

People appreciate being given options. Problems make customers feel overwhelmed and powerless, especially in a government setting, since resources are limited and timelines are strict. Giving them a clear set of options provides them with the power to make decisions best suited to their needs.

When there are limited resources or budget restrictions, you might have to work with the customer to find alternative ways to meet their goals. To keep the customer engaged, offer choices to help them meet their priorities without losing sight of the bigger picture.

For instance, if an employee cannot continue in their full-time role due to personal reasons but is still valuable to the project, ask about offering them the option to reduce their hours or adjust their responsibilities. Present a potential solution to the customer like this:

"One of our team members can no longer continue in their full-time role due to personal circumstances. However, I've proposed the possibility of keeping them on part-time to ensure continued support for key tasks. This would allow us to maintain critical services while accommodating their needs. Would you be open to discussing this option?"

This approach empowers the customer, making them feel in control of the situation. Involving them increases the likelihood they will say "yes" to your proposal or at least feel they've had a say in the decision.

Making Difficult Situations Work in a Strained Environment

Government support often happens in a resource-constrained environment, where employees are asked to do more with less. Hiring freezes, budget cuts, or changing priorities make it difficult to meet customer expectations. However, the key to success is to find creative solutions that can still meet the customer's needs. You can wallow in the constraints, or you can do something about it.

In such strained environments, flexibility and adaptability are vital. If you know a customer is facing budget cuts but still has critical needs, it's helpful to approach the situation with ideas that fit within the limits. Some ways to do this are to offer part-time staffing options, propose task re-prioritization, or suggest partnerships with other departments. None of these solutions requires immediate additional funding, but they still provide value.

Long-Term Success through Collaboration

Communication is the foundation of success. It's not just about delivering services; it's about creating and maintaining positive, collaborative customer relationships. Be clear, direct, empathetic, and solution-oriented to navigate challenging situations with your customers and help them feel supported. The best government professionals understand the human side of their roles and use their expertise to create positive, lasting relationships.

Strive to offer solutions, maintain transparency, and create a cooperative atmosphere— the customer's trust and satisfaction will naturally follow. Over time, this approach will ensure individual success as well as the success of your organization, allowing both you and the customer to thrive, even in a challenging environment.

SWOT ANALYSIS SHEET

STRENGTHS	WEAKNESSES

OPPORTUNITIES	THREATS

CHAPTER 23

Tools

"Give us the tools, and we will finish the job."

— WINSTON CHURCHILL, "GIVE US THE TOOLS" (1941)[43]

Leadership involves putting out fires, meeting assigned leadership duties, and upholding every requirement your job entails—and the right tools will maximize your time, efficiency, and success in each sphere. Balancing everything—the job requirements, leadership requirements, and tasks you discover while interacting with employees—can be a major challenge for leaders.

It's good practice to regularly ask yourself, "How am I managing my time? How am I maximizing tools to save time? How can I complete everything expected of me?" A leader's goal should be to understand the available tools, understand which tools could be needed, and understand which tools would be most valuable at any given moment.

The True Tool for Success

There's one tool you can't do without if you want to succeed—you (and you'd better be sharp)! Yes, I'm calling you a tool. Don't worry—I don't mean it in a bad way. Let me see if I can dig my way out of this. (I'm going to need a big shovel!) When I say you're a tool, I'm talking about your skills, your shortcomings, and your ability to handle the ups and downs of your business. Your skills will obviously be needed, but you'll also need to be aware of your shortcomings to choose employees who can fill the gaps you leave. Resilience—the ability to handle the ups and downs—is also critical and will carry you far beyond your current role.

I faced several challenges (or resilience-growing moments) as a leader. Some of them include disappointments from seeing strong applicants I ultimately couldn't hire, frustration from being unable to influence prime contractors' response times and the government's decision-making processes, and inconsistency of information and capabilities across contracts. Self-managing the ups and downs will enable you to stay engaged and move forward consistently. Doing this will contribute to your success as well as the success of your company.

Keep Your Toolkit Handy

The purpose of our tools is to make customers' and employees' lives easier. Keep your toolkit close to ensure communication while supporting the employee and the customer. Helpful tools for employee needs include simple-to-use HR engagements for training, tuition assistance programs, straightforward time-keeping, and corporate processes such as travel approvals or healthcare information.

Here are some standard constructs you can use to engage with and help employees:
- A "first day on the job" checklist to show who the employee reports to in the government and at the contract company
- Calendar reminders for deliverable due dates
- Leave trackers and hour trackers to ensure they're on pace and not over their hours on the contract

These tools will free up your brain power so you can handle the tough challenges coming your way. You don't have to create them all; you just need to be the one making them available. It's your responsibility to ensure employees have the right tools at the right time.

Here are your options:
- Create tools/templates
- Leverage tools/templates you've seen before
- Get the company to create tools/templates

Tools are always evolving. They add to your ability to be a good teammate, leader, or manager, but a tool is only as good as its use. You could get the best tool in existence, and if your employees don't use it, you've just wasted your money. Tools add zero value to your team unless your team utilizes them.

Startup, Midsize, and Enterprise Company Tools

The tools your company uses will often depend on the size of the company. As I've said before, what makes sense at one time may not make sense at another time. Startups are smaller and tend to have limited financial resources, while enterprise companies have more financial resources but less time to spend on manual tasks. Midsize companies are outgrowing the startup model but aren't as big as enterprise companies.

Maybe you're thinking, "The right tool changes based on company size— great! But what does that actually look like?" Here's an example: A small startup can easily use a spreadsheet to track travel or vacation time. It takes hardly any time, especially if you have one employee who travels once a year. As the company grows, though, you'll need more, so you transition it to a SharePoint list website the entire team can use to track travel. If you've got even more resources, you can create a widget within the Customer Relationship Management (CRM) tool.

With a CRM widget, enterprise companies can track:
- Cost breakdowns
- Vacation/Travel locations
- The time between travel approval and vacation reporting, etc.

Specific Tools You Can Use At Each Growth Stage

Here are some tools you can use (if needed) based on your company size and what you do.

Startup/Small Team Tools

- Trello/Asana/ClickUp
- Training Trackers (ADP, Excel, etc.)
- Outlook Buttons and Task Reminders

Midsize/Growing Company Tools
- Monday/Smartsheet/Wrike
- SharePoint/Teams/Cloud (Box.com)
- MS Project for High-Resource Tasks
- Briefings for Contract Information Tracking
- CRM/UNANET Automated Reports

Large/Enterprise Company Tools
- NetSuite/SAP/Oracle
- CRM/Unanet automated reports
- Excel with Macros and Pivot Tables

Unconventional Tools

An item I view as a tool many may disagree with me on is a meeting. The goal of a meeting is to quickly enable the sharing of information—it sounds like a tool to me! The challenge is to ensure the meeting aligns with a requirement and is needed to meet the requirement. Bottom line: it's got to add value. Don't hold a meeting just to get everyone together in the same room—hold a meeting to reduce other meetings, phone calls, or emails.

My meeting policy is to either provide the same information to a wide group of people quickly and efficiently or allow everyone to engage so I can ensure they're getting the support they need. The right meeting at the right time with the right people can save time, reduce confusion, and save money for a company. Too many meetings can cut into the company's time and money, so strike the right balance to avoid getting "This could have been an email" messages from people.

One last note about meetings: I don't personally like daily tag-ups, but they make sense in some contexts. For example, daily or twice-daily meetings could make sense if you're building a software program with multiple coders. It doesn't make sense, though, if you're giving month-end deliverable reviews to the government.

Another unconventional tool is a saying my mentor gave me that's enabled me to evaluate tools: "Kill stupid." Feels aggressive to kill stupid, but he had a point. Plenty of tasks we do every day are stupid, not thought through, and not beneficial to our goals. Some stupid things you have to put up with—they're part of business, or rules set forth to test your willingness to endure stupidity. Other things are stupid of our own making—decisions that seemed smart at the time or processes that worked amazingly when you had just five employees, but are downright stupid now that you've got 20 or 200 employees.

The point of "kill stupid" is to remind you to look at what you do and ensure it still makes sense today. Are your processes getting in the way of doing tasks efficiently? When you kill stupid, you stay open to change (not for the sake of change itself, but for the betterment of the situation, process, or structure).

I had the opportunity to kill stupid when I realized a team was using a PDF fillable document for approvals to move money around. When the PDF was created, it was a requirement—a smart way to ensure approvals had a flow and couldn't be changed by people downstream. As time went on, a new system was implemented—a workflow automation enabling people to get approvals within the system. This part of the system wasn't being used because people were still using the PDF. Their process used the PDF to get approvals, upload it into the system, and then redo the entire process, minus a few people who weren't in the system.

I asked around to see how hard it'd be to add new users, ask if it'd cost more money to use the system, and see how easy it'd be to build new workflows in the system. Turned out to be a free fix that eliminated the need to email a PDF, shaving three days off their previous approval cycle and removing the risk of non-system errors (since everything had to be manually entered into the PDF). Though the PDF made sense at first, it became stupid over time. I was able to "kill stupid" by seeing an opportunity and taking the initiative to get it done.

Action Step

Review your company's processes. Are there some tasks that used to make sense and don't anymore? Take the time to kill stupid today—your company will thank you for it later!

REMEMBER

The purpose of our tools is to make customers' and employees' lives easier.

SWOT ANALYSIS SHEET

STRENGTHS	WEAKNESSES

OPPORTUNITIES	THREATS

CHAPTER 24

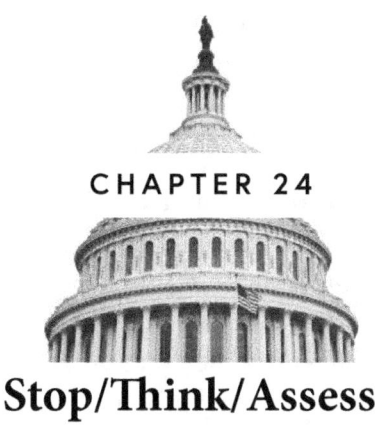

Stop/Think/Assess

"...Before you write, think... Before you criticize, wait...
Before you quit, try..."

—WILLIAM ARTHUR WARD, "BEFORE YOU" [44]

You're busy. Sometimes it feels like you don't have time to eat lunch, let alone think of the items of the day. If you don't think about what's going on around you, though, you won't see the gaps or notice when a challenge is headed your way. This means you can't be proactive, only reactive, which is not good since it's usually easier to prevent a problem than to fix one. Most problems become personal or emotional. For instance, it's easier to keep someone from thinking they're a failure than it is to reverse the damage after they already think they are one.

Leaders in the government world deal with personnel issues more than anything else. There are more personnel issues than issues with deliverables, cost overruns, scheduling challenges, or technical challenges. Of course, leaders handle all these other problems too, but people are the number one concern for leaders. Sometimes, people-centered problems are actually training problems, tool problems, or other problems that would be clearer if the leader took a step back and looked at the big picture. Putting stop/think/assess into practice now can save you hours of problems later.

Stop

The next time you're confronted with a problem, take a breath and think about the tasks, paths, and challenges ahead. Don't take action immediately—stop for a moment. Responding immediately to an email might feel like you're getting the job done, but will responding too quickly mean more work for you later? Will it require more work from someone else? I can't tell you how many times someone reads an email and takes immediate action without thinking to look through the rest of the emails in their inbox to see if there's an update. Sometimes the answers to the questions you're asking are there, just in a separate email. This could happen because the sender didn't read through all of their emails either, and now they're sending you new information they could have consolidated into one email. This could also happen because there's new information, but whatever the reason, this is one of the ways wires get crossed.

It's tempting to act immediately instead of asking questions or looking at the bigger picture. Instead, you should read the email twice, ask a question to validate the need, and start thinking about the requirement you're working on before you take action. Most of the phone calls I get are from people who didn't read the entire email but think they know what to do. If you take time to think about the need in front of you, though, it'll actually *save* your time and your team's time. Don't make any "per my last email" gremlins and don't become one—read twice, and reply once!

Still not convinced why you should stop when you could respond as quickly as possible? Here are some reasons:

- **When you stop, you take control instead of being swept away by the moment.** You can navigate the issues with a clear head instead of being controlled by outward circumstances.

- **One minute now could save you 10 minutes later.** A quick response isn't thought out and won't have all the needed information. Taking a minute (or a day) to plan projects out will save time and contribute toward better communication.

- **Time minimizes your emotional response.** Sometimes you'll read an email and need to take a walk around the building. Sometimes you'll draft a response and let it sit for a moment, only to come back and fully rewrite it.

Emotion is the enemy of clear and concise communication. Stop before you hit "reply," and it could save a relationship.

Think

You need time to think out a response. If you're responding to an email, reply by saying you've received the message and will send the answer shortly. If you're in person, write down the need or question with as much detail as possible and let the other person know you've written it down, and you'll respond soon. (Tell them how long you think it'll be—manage their expectations.) Then mull the issue over... reread the email if the problem was brought up in an email, or reread your notes. Think about the short-term and long-term possibilities, and realize no answer you give will be 100% perfect. Consider the challenges, request the amount of time you'll need to think through them, and then act on the best solutions.

Taking time to think helps clarify these questions:
- Why am I being asked this?
- Why is this response important?
- What will happen when I respond?

In any situation, there are multiple approaches you can take. When you consider these questions, you can develop a plan of attack most suited to your specific situation.

Assess

You took the time to stop, thought about what you were going to do, and then went with what you thought the best outcome would be. Now it's time to assess.

Think about the positives and negatives of the decision you made:
- Look at what happened
- Think about why it happened
- Consider how it's ended up now

Ask yourself, "Did this go how I thought it would, or did it go off the rails? Did the path I chose create other unexpected outcomes?" Use the data you get from these reflections to make stronger, faster, more informed decisions in the future. No decision is perfect—it'll have second and third-level effects you didn't see coming that may shock you. Hopefully, as you advance in your career, the shocking moments will happen less often, but they'll still be there.

You're in the people business, and taking stock of decisions is important. Ask yourself:
- Did I make a good choice?
- Did I talk to the right people to make a good choice?
- If the outcome is the same next time, will I still make this choice?
- Did I communicate well? Did I create misunderstandings?
- Are the wrong people in the wrong places?

The amount of time between your initial decision and the assessment will vary. If you just ate a chocolate bar from a candy bowl and realized the bowl isn't refilled often (because the candy's old and stale), you can assess it right away. Your assessment might sound like, "I'm not eating chocolate from their candy bowl anymore!" Other decisions—like assessing a new hire—will take time. Generally speaking, it's normal to wait until 90 days after a new hire to evaluate the employee's performance.

The Ongoing Cycle of Stop/Think/Assess

The process of continually stopping, thinking, and assessing will enable you to understand yourself and grow into a better leader and person. Looking back at where you've been helps you see the road ahead. Reflecting on past experiences enables you to avoid future roadblocks.

Revisit this chapter regularly to think about:
- What works
- What doesn't work
- How to talk to people
- How to build briefings
- How to finish paperwork
- How to be early for due dates (or not, since waiting sometimes has value)
- How to manage the expectations of the people around you

The stop/think/assess cycle will help you take control of your work and decisions. It forces you to break free of rushed decisions and knee-jerk reactions, creating a feedback loop for success that will help at work and in your personal life. You'll react with a sense of calm, build better relationships, and enhance your ability to learn from situations, thereby increasing your efficiency and reducing your stress.

I know you're busy, but don't fall into a cycle of reactivity. Instead, take the time to stop, think, and assess. When you do, you'll become more balanced, healthy, thoughtful, and productive.

Action Step

Think back on a recent decision you made. Follow the "assess" steps to determine if the decision you made was a good one, a bad one, or one you could improve upon. What will you do differently next time? How will you remember to stop/think/assess the next time you need to make a decision?

SWOT ANALYSIS SHEET

STRENGTHS	WEAKNESSES

OPPORTUNITIES	THREATS

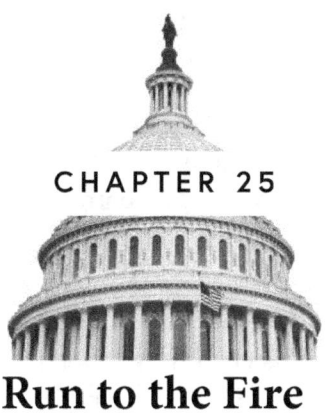

CHAPTER 25

Run to the Fire

"The best way out is always through."

—ROBERT FROST, A SERVANT TO SERVANTS [45]

Bad news never gets better. A spark doesn't go out on its own—you must take action. Leaders look for the fires, run to them, and engage them immediately. How do you see the fires? By communicating often (and often, too often)! Engage with your customers and employees to see the sparks that are kindled into a blaze when left unchecked. If you're not looking, the spark will quickly become an inferno, and many of your options will be off the table by then. A leader who seems not to respond to bad news by taking action will be negatively perceived, and their contract management skills will be in question. This can end up on your contract performance record (preventing you from getting additional work) and can hurt contract ratings.

A Real-Life Example of Avoiding the Fire

At the beginning of the book, I talked about an incident motivating me to write this book, but I want to provide more detail and context so you can get a better understanding of the multiple cases where those responsible failed to run to the fire. I was a program manager and the company I worked for was a subcontractor. We had five employees on the contract, one of which was the team lead. In this contract, the team lead was the central point of contact for contract questions like travel requests, leave tracking, day-to-day employee questions, etc. The prime contractor had the majority of the workforce on the contract and knew the team lead was the go-to person for needs within the office. My job was to provide final engagement and approval of the subcontract to prime engagements, but again, most day-to-day tasks were handled by the team lead.

One day, I got a forwarded email from the prime which originally came from the government. This email was addressed to the prime and stated they wanted to remove an employee for poor performance, lack of communication, and failure to uphold the requirement to be in the office one day each week. (This email was the first I heard of any issues. Before then, I had regular conversations with the prime, asking if any issues needed to be addressed, and no negative feedback was shared with me.) The email contained a list of dates the employee was absent from the office, revealed proof of a lack of timely communication from the employee (timestamps, etc.), and listed other concerns.

I called up the prime contractor and learned the prime got an email from the government two weeks earlier, stating they were concerned about the employee's performance and wanted to talk about how to provide high-quality support. The email went unanswered—maybe because the prime didn't think the email was urgent, then forgot about it—and two weeks later the government sent the termination email. By then, we'd lost all our ability to influence the government and fix any issues, real or imagined. The decision was already made. No one put out the first spark, and the fire became inevitable.

I had to suspend the employee and investigate whether the government's allegations were valid. During my investigation, I learned the government had also communicated with a prime contract team lead, but the team lead didn't share the information with the project manager. The government also didn't share concerns with the employee in a clear enough way to compel the employee to make significant changes to their government interactions.

This fire didn't have to happen. There could have been another outcome if things had been different. If the team lead had brought the concerns up to me, I could have asked questions and brought the employee into my office at least two weeks before the government sent the second email to voice their concerns. If the team lead and prime project manager had run to the fire instead of letting it blaze out of control, we could have increased our communication, oversight, and support to this employee and potentially saved their job. Instead, the spark became a fire, and the fire turned into a firing—we had to let the employee go. It didn't end there. The government wasn't happy, so when we put a new resume forward for the position, the government told us the position was put on hold for backfill based on requirement reviews. Failure to run to the fire cost someone their job, cost the company a position, and created a negative experience for the government customer. One of our jobs is to keep the government out of trouble, and this situation caused them trouble.

Lessons Learned From Avoiding the Fire

Though it was painful, this incident taught me many lessons:

1. **Don't assume everyone knows what to do and how to do it.** We had a team lead on-site, and if we had ensured the employee was properly trained, they would have known to run to the fire.

2. **Expand on training for team leads.** I ensured this wouldn't happen again by giving the team leads the right tools in the right places so they'd have them at the right time.

3. **Ensure everyone knows the organizational chart and points of contact for each contract.** The government employee who was having issues with the contractor was meeting frequently with the subcontractor team lead for lunch, but had no idea the person they were meeting with was responsible for the employee. If they had, everyone could have communicated sooner, and the issue could have been solved before it was too late.

4. **Stress the importance of communication to all team members.** Because I didn't do this, the team lead didn't know to check in with the government every month to see if there were any needs or issues with employees.

5. **This event was the result of many errors.** I failed to lead the team, and the team lead failed to lean forward to ensure employee success. The prime team lead failed to communicate up the chain of command, and the prime project manager failed to take action after receiving the first email voicing the government's concerns.

You Have a Team—Act Like It

You don't need to take anything on alone—no emergency, no challenge, no oddity needs to be handled solo. You can use a team to navigate issues. If an employee is not performing to standard on a government on-site location and the government is concerned about it, lean on HR training to navigate the situation.

There are specific steps you should take to notify employees about their performance. Everything has to be documented to ensure the company is tracking the issue—whether the path is to rectify the issue or let the employee go. Failure to document appropriately makes it much harder to terminate an employee if it gets to that point.

Annual reviews are also more difficult without documentation. Not everything requiring a team's help will involve employee challenges. Assistance with contracts is another good reason to call in a team—if a contract is running out of funds, you'll need to communicate it to the government or the prime contractor you're supporting.

Other Considerations

On Relationships

Some relationships are easy and open—the customer is always ahead of funding needs and communicates them. Not all customer relationships work this way, though. Sometimes, you have to follow contract rules closely to keep the government in the loop. You may need to rely on the contracts manager to ensure you don't do anything you shouldn't. They may also need to let you know you're missing something, like a "75% Expended" letter. (A "75% Expended" letter is given to the government from the company to let them know the funds for a contract are 75% expended. These letters are important for communication and to alert the government funds are running out, so no one is surprised or has to send employees home because they didn't know contract funds were dwindling.)

Intent to Exercise the Option of a Contract

When transitioning from one option year of a contract to the next, the government has to send an "Intent to Exercise the Option of a Contract" letter 30 days before the expiration period of the current contract. If this doesn't happen, it can cause a lot of stress to employees who thought they were in a secure position and now have to look for work. Don't deal with these moments alone—work with leadership, contracts, and HR to navigate moments that can cost people their jobs if you aren't proactive.

Don't Cover Anything Up

Everything eventually comes to light in government contracting. Open and honest communication usually ends positively. No one's perfect.

No Contract is Perfect

One of my favorite sayings from the beginning of my contract specialist days was "You're always one contract mod away from a perfect contract." I've never actually seen a perfect contract, but luckily, a contract doesn't have to be perfect before you can execute it. That doesn't mean I haven't seen contracts get terminated. Most contracts are terminated because they've become inconvenient for the government, either because the requirement wasn't needed due to changes in technology or because costs were too high with little benefit.

Keep Learning

Pay attention to details, lean on your team, and be open and honest. The fires will go out (and then be replaced by new ones).

REMEMBER

Bad news never gets better. A spark doesn't go out on its own—you must take action. Leaders look for the fires, run to them, and engage them immediately.

SWOT ANALYSIS SHEET

STRENGTHS	WEAKNESSES

OPPORTUNITIES	THREATS

CHAPTER 26

Company Growth Mindset

"Growth is never by mere chance; it is the result of forces working together."

— ATTRIBUTED TO JAMES CASH PENNEY [46]

Growth isn't luck or magic, it's getting people to row the boat in the same direction. It's creating a shared vision of the future. You grow by creating trust, shared effort, shared service, and shared success. No matter where you are in your career, think about growth for you and the company you support. Consider what you want to improve. Push boundaries and build a bigger future for you and the company.

If you're a leader, your reputation will get around. People will talk about how you are with customers and employees. It's part of your "other duties as assigned," whether you want to believe it or not. We all want to be viewed positively (both in our professional lives and our personal lives). We all want to help people grow—to open doors for our companies, ourselves, and other people. One of the best ways to get your name out there is by serving others. After all, we are in the customer service profession!

As your reputation gets around, people will decide—right or wrong— whether you have integrity, whether you are trustworthy, and if you have the backs of your employees, from the newest in the company to the original hire by the owner. They'll discuss whether you provide solid support to the company you work for and to the government you support. People's beliefs about you will impact your growth and the growth of your company. If people believe you are a good teammate, they will want you as a teammate. They'll help you get more positions on contracts and more employees.

Remember: people always talk. Everything you're doing every day builds your reputation. It's either helping or hurting you and your company. You don't have to be perfect, but you do have to be real.

Ask People

When communicating with employees, customers, or your network, ask people if they need help. If you're a sub on a contract, asking might create a network of engagement increasing your work (by putting more people on a contract), but if you don't ask, you can't find the gaps. Finding the gaps where people need help is how we start to grow.

If you don't ask what you can do for the customer, the employees, or the company, you'll end up
 making assumptions instead. Why assume when you can know their opinions? Not every answer is going to be a golden road to victory, but every response will give you a little more information. Every question you ask will give the people around you more opportunities to open the door to communication.

As an employee, you asked your manager what help they needed, and you should continue to ask your leadership whether they need help. As a manager, you should ask your employees what help they need. As a leader on a contract, you should ask the government what items they need.

Here are some good questions to ask (whether you're an employee, a leader, or a manager):
- Are you getting everything you need?
- Where can I help you?
- What am I missing?
- What's next on your plate?

Don't assume—ask.

The more you ask, the more gaps you identify, and the more opportunities you have to be the filler for those gaps. You will create more value for yourself, your employees, and your company by filling the gaps. There are always opportunities within program offices to consolidate requirements or expand them, to create streamlined processes, and to enable the workforce to become more engaged and standardized. It is possible to stay within the bounds of a contract and work in the gray area of support at the same time.

How to Grow

As the company grows, you grow. You might not get a promotion immediately, but you'll learn new skills, gain experience, take on new responsibilities, and build your resume. If all goes to plan, you will eventually get a promotion, and with it, more money. Do you think promotions will just happen to you? Think again. You always have to chase the next raise, opportunity, or stepping stone toward your career. Positions allowing for natural growth are rare—you'll have to force the issue from time to time.

Because positions allowing for natural growth are rare, it's also rare to stay within the same company. You change, positions change, opportunities change, and where you'll need to go to grow changes. Don't feel bad for wanting to grow and chase opportunities, but remember growth takes time. If you want to run the company someday, learning the steps along the way will give you the experience to do it. Focusing on company growth will help you get the next promotion, level of responsibility, and experience to get to your ideal (final) position.

Be ready, though—as you grow, you may find your ideal position isn't ideal after all. Maybe you'll start out wanting to be a CEO and then discover you fit better as a senior-level manager or vice president. Remember my picture of a career path at the start of this book? It's okay (and normal) if your path has many twists and turns. The good thing about this book is taking the steps to learn the ropes might help you find out you are closer to your ideal position than you thought. If a lower-stress position can bring as much joy into your work and life as a high-stress position, why not take it?

Step one of growth is to serve. If you want to get noticed as an employee, a leader, or a company, be the one who is always up front, serving the greater good without their hand out for more. Are you going to get more work for the company or money for yourself every time you step up front and offer help? No. But it does help build your reputation. It lets people know you are a team player. It shows the world you can be counted on. Serve the greater good now and get more later—more responsibility, more respect, more money.

Don't forget, not all growth is up. Over time, my waist has gotten wider, and so has my skillset. I did not stay in the lane of a contract specialist. I worked as a financial analyst, an acquisition analyst, and a program integrator. I got wider in my knowledge, and that gave me the ability to speak many "languages" across the silos of government support. Knowing what others do and communicating strongly with those skill sets eventually enabled me to grow vertically into program management. Growth takes time and the willingness to learn. Chasing a promotion for yourself (or the next contract for the company) takes time, growth, and respect from those around you. Throwing your hat in the ring is important—you can't get told yes or no without trying—but having the right boxes checked to get a "yes" is a key factor in success.

Bringing Ideas to Leadership

Don't take it personally if you bring a groundbreaking idea to leadership and they say no. Companies are constantly changing and are always communicating. Good companies learn from today and from the past to create a stronger future. Good companies want to hear ideas that can help the company grow, be more profitable, get their names out there, etc. However, companies also have finite resources, limited time, or other agreements in place, so the best ideas to streamline or fix things might not be doable at this time.

Bringing ideas is part of your job, and you should bring as many ideas to the company as you can—just don't expect them to be executed. Sometimes, the company will tell you why an idea wasn't actionable. Use this information to build actionable ideas.

Here's the cycle you should aim for:
- Bring ideas
- Hear "no"
- Learn why they said "no"
- Tweak the idea and bring new ideas

Bottom line: expect to hear "no" and don't be discouraged by it. Keep bringing ideas. A "no" today might be a "yes" in a year if the landscape changes and the reason they said "no" is not valid anymore.

Turning a "No" into a "Yes"

Turning a "no" into a "yes" is extremely difficult to accomplish. Sometimes the "no" is because of nothing more than bad timing, and a year from now, your idea about bringing the new system into the company or the new SharePoint website into the program office is going to take off. A year could bring additional resources or changes in leadership. It could even give you time to build your skills and create a beta on your own to "show" the tool instead of just talking about the concept.

In one of the offices I supported, the leadership was using a specific system with had a ton more capability than they were using. They were taking extra time and effort doing a lot of tasks outside of the system instead of doing them within the system. All it would take is a few simple edits to the routing. However, I was the new guy—I hadn't built personal trust in the office yet. The first time I discussed the solution, my leadership said, "Our process works right now."

About six months later, the process had an error. A requirement needed to be funded quickly, but a lot of people were on leave or travel, and the process they had in place required signatures on a document before the document could be put in the system to route it for approval a second time.

I brought up the idea again at this moment—the moment of failure— and this time the leadership said, "Let's beta the idea in your group." I got my "yes." Within a few days, I worked with the technical group to update the system to allow a single internal approval workflow, and we rolled out the test. It worked great! It took review and approval time down from over a week to only a few hours. It also got rid of document and email chains and duplication of approvals and workflows. Now the entire office uses it. Sometimes a great idea gets a "no" at first, then gets a shot and works. Don't take the "no" personally.

Be the Driver of Growth!

If you get nothing else from this chapter, realize you are the only person in your life who can drive your growth. You might be part of a team to help the company grow, but you have to force your growth alongside the company's growth.

Growth doesn't just happen; the elements have to be right. You have to have personal drive, leadership that will listen, employees who are in the right places, government opportunities to expand into, and a thousand other factors all have to fall into place. However, you can focus on forcing those elements, creating the right circumstances, and taking advantage of the battlefield you have laid out.

Be the person to help others. Be the person who learns, adapts, and asks the questions. Be the person with the energy and focus to succeed for yourself, your employees, and your company. Build the career you are proud of, the team that lasts, and the company that wins!

REMEMBER

If you get nothing else from this chapter, realize you are the only person in your life who can drive your growth. That is worth repeating!

SWOT ANALYSIS SHEET

STRENGTHS	WEAKNESSES

OPPORTUNITIES	THREATS

CHAPTER 27

Everyone Falls… Now What?

"Change is inevitable—except from a vending machine."

— ORIGIN UNKNOWN [47]

When I was learning to play hockey in 2016, I fell on my knees over and over. I realized they're stronger than I thought! Back then, I said to myself, "Hockey is awesome. I get exercise, a legal way to let out my aggression, camaraderie, and the motivation to get better." It wasn't all sunshine, though. The first time I fell, I could have crawled away, saying skating was too hard. If I'd done that, I'd have never grown to enjoy the sport like I do today.

In 2022, I had the worst fall I've ever been through, resulting in a non-contact ACL and meniscus tear. I had to have my ACL replaced with my PCL and a harpoon installed in my meniscus. I could've stopped playing hockey. I could've said, "Well, crap. I'm almost 40—time to stop acting like a 20-year-old and start sitting on my couch all day."

Instead, I began the recovery process so I could play again. Maybe I'm dumb… maybe I just like hitting people without getting into trouble for it… Maybe I just hate running, and hockey's more fun. It took about two years to get back to "almost myself," and I have to wear a brace now. It's been a hard road mentally, seeing how fast health can be taken away. But I get back up after every fall because it keeps me young, motivated, and moving forward in life.

Falls Happen

So I fell playing hockey—why am I telling you this? Because falls happen in our personal lives and our work lives. It's how you respond to them that counts. If you fall in your career, take ownership. It's just a matter of time before you fall, even if you have all the tools you need, communicate daily with every employee, and ask the customer every day about their needs. You don't find out who a person is in the good times—you learn their character in the bad times. Be a good person and realize the worst time you can imagine now will only help you grow.

Is Leadership Right for You?

It's hard to manage your personal life and then have to "manage" others' (work) lives too—so what do you do? This book was created to help you mitigate some of the imperfect situations you'll encounter, but it won't get rid of all possible problems. Is being a leader worth it to you? It's not for everyone. Sometimes it's more about timing than anything else—remember my five-year break? The concept of stop/think/assess is real. It lets you see what's going on around you and make real judgments about where you are and where you want to be, mapping out the way to get there.

Moments of Growth

Some of the biggest moments of growth in my life haven't been from success, but from having things go completely off the rails. The communication issues leading up to letting an employee go are a good example. In the moments that feel like I'm getting punched in the face, I learn more about myself, my wants in life, my goals for employees and the company, and my willingness to be a leader than I do when work is running smoothly.

When life goes smoothly, you get a false sense of knowing and having control over everything. You start thinking nothing can go wrong because you run a perfect ship. It's only when the truth comes—that no matter how perfect the ship is, the world is always changing and sometimes the hurricane crashes into your ship and sinks it—that you realize you've got to start swimming, keep your head above water, and find a new ship.

Or don't.

I know this is a weird comment to make in a book about being a strong employee and leader, but it's true—not all people are leaders. (If you're not sure you want to lead, feel free to skip to "Are You Sure? Part Two.") Learning who you are and what you want by gaining knowledge and experience isn't failure; it's growth. Don't let any expectation (whether it's a person's expectation or a societal/cultural one) force you into a life you're not happy with. Becoming a top-performing employee can be as high-paying and rewarding as leadership, but without the struggle of being responsible for other people. Don't be afraid to go back to an employee role after gaining leadership knowledge and experience. You may find it rebuilds your confidence, enables you to be a better employee, and gives you the time to determine whether you'd like to pursue a leadership role in the future. You don't have to go through life according to other people's timetables—you determine where you go in life.

Lessons from Falling

I hate falling. I don't know anyone who enjoys it. Falling has taught me some valuable lessons, though:

1. **You can't control everything.** You only have so much time in your day, and only so much time in your life. If you're focused on controlling everything, you're going to exhaust yourself only to find there are still things beyond your control.

2. **Sometimes you have to make an imperfect decision.** Sometimes you'll choose a course of action that creates challenges, but moves the ball down the field. It could cause more work now, but following the 80% rule can cause movement that will result in finding a solution.

3. **Remember the 80% rule.** If you've never heard of it, the 80% rule states 80% of actions get you the most gains in a decision. This

means the final 20% is less productive and can sometimes be left out entirely. This doesn't work in every situation—writing policies, for example—but an item within the policy can still be useful if it's only 80% developed.

4. **Falling down can be a strong learning opportunity.** Sometimes you jump into a task, learn 80% of it, and then learn what you did wrong and how to fix it. That is a better lesson than trying to get it perfect. If you wait for 100% perfection, you may learn your solution isn't 100% after all. Falling might actually be more productive—use it as a tool to get stronger, and you'll hopefully fall less.

REMEMBER

*Falls happen in our personal
lives and our work lives. It's
how you respond to them that
counts. If you fall in your career,
take ownership.*

SWOT ANALYSIS SHEET

STRENGTHS	WEAKNESSES

OPPORTUNITIES	THREATS

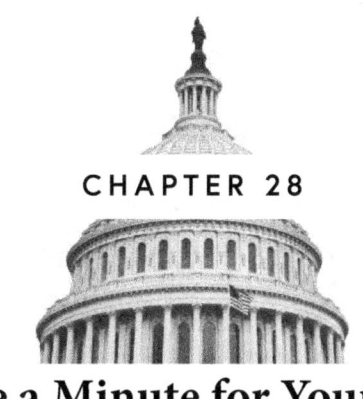

CHAPTER 28

Take a Minute for Yourself

"Nature does not hurry, yet everything is accomplished."

— LAO TZU [48]

Turn off your phone, log off your email, and recharge from time to time. You get vacation time added to every paycheck—use it! Remembering why you work and taking rest to increase your motivation to work are as important as the work itself. As much as you can, plan your time proactively so your time away can be seamless. It's better to build out your schedule early with regular and consistent breaks than to take on too much work all at once, hit a wall, and require immediate time away.

Sometimes, you will have to drop everything to take care of yourself and your family. Don't feel bad about it—those pauses are unavoidable, and it's important to take care of the larger part of your life. Unexpected deaths and illnesses are just that—unexpected. Take the time you need to take care of yourself or your family and don't feel guilty about taking time away. Companies hire humans, not robots. The time off is necessary, and it's there for those moments in your life. At other moments, though, you'll have time to plan breaks into your work and schedule.

Managing Stress

I've been fortunate not to have to worry about how breaks will negatively impact my work when I get back. The stress of taking a break only to worry about making up the time or wondering if work is piling up is real. You return after your vacation feeling rested and relaxed, only to find you need to spend the next two weeks fixing what people broke while you were out. The stress from wondering whether work is going well at the office while on vacation can't be fully removed, but it can be minimized.

Here are some of the practical ways you can reduce stress ahead of a vacation:

- **Think ahead.** Consider spreading out your vacation time so you take several small vacations every couple of months. (Think of this as a proactive way to prevent burnout!) If you plan it right, it'll be like taking a quick breath of fresh air just before overwhelm starts to hit you.

- **Set up back-ups to manage needs.** Put people in charge of specific tasks, projects, or responsibilities while you're out. Train them a week or two before, or create and leave helpful resources so they can do the job well.

- **Plan your vacation at the right time.** If possible, plan your vacation during a natural slow point. This will enable you to truly disconnect instead of returning to an overstuffed email inbox. (Note: This is not always doable, but if it is, you will have a more restful vacation.)

Other Ways to Take Time for Yourself

Going on vacation and turning off your phone aren't the only ways to set aside time for yourself. Start by learning what gives you meaning, calms you down, creates value, and gets you excited. Personally, I like playing golf and hockey. I'm in leagues for both sports, and it's turned into a weekly requirement that I "relax." I'm forced to unplug and focus on myself (and the game) for a bit. I enjoy these two because of the physical activity and competitive aspects—it's impossible to think about other things while I'm doing them because all my focus needs to be on what I'm doing. Your hobbies might be different—painting, sewing, drawing, chess—just make sure you continually recharge to continue to participate in the marathon of work.

Dangers of Not Taking a Break

I've seen people who were consumed by work and stress. They sat behind a desk for 12 hours a day and then gained 100 pounds because they didn't have time to take care of themselves. I've seen people let their mental and physical health fall by the wayside and die young. I don't want that for you, and I don't want it for myself.

I've made the mistake of not prioritizing my well-being. I hated everything: going to work, interacting with my coworkers, and doing my job. It cost me personal happiness and professional relationships. It wasn't until later I realized a lot of my mistakes were my own doing. When I finally figured out how to work, play, relax, learn continually, and not take things personally, I was able to succeed in multiple areas of life.

Remember: work is only a part of our lives. If we don't take time for ourselves and the people around us, we might never make it to retirement or whatever we want to do. If we do make it to our professional goals but neglect the people around us, we might have no one to celebrate it with. Instead, balance doing what pays your bills with what fuels your life—the people who make all the hard work worthwhile—so you can look back one day and say you got everything out of life you wanted from it.

Work-Life Balance: Does it Exist?

I personally don't believe in work/life balance. To me, it means you're either doing one or the other, but I feel like I take care of work at home and vice versa. My goal isn't to keep them separate—it's to manage the merging of the two. I feel calmer when I stay engaged with both sides at the same time. Whether my break is a cruise or a dental appointment, I keep my work email on my phone so I don't return to 100 emails in my inbox.

Not everyone is willing or able to merge work and home, and that's okay. You can separate your work and personal time if it works for you. Do whatever you need to do to keep from being overwhelmed and stressed. Choose the most healthy method for you—the one that will safeguard you from wanting to run away from it all.

Visualize Your Goals

Remember earlier, when I said to think about your "why," or the reason you want to be a government contractor? Take some extra time now to visualize your goals, understand your "why," and imagine a perfect day. What do you do on this perfect day? What are your goals? Why do you choose to get up and go to work every morning? Everyone's answers to these questions will be different, but they're important questions to think about.

Action Step

If you haven't thought of your "why" or your long-term goals already, now is a perfect opportunity. Think of your life in 10-year increments. For example, think about what you want your life to be like at age 40, age 50, and age 60. Write down what you expect from each decade (both personally and professionally). Go ahead—do it now. I can wait.

Got it? Good. Now, take a look at the list and think about the goals you had for yourself when you were a teenager. Did your 20s go the way you expected them to go? Chances are they didn't. Life rarely goes as planned. Even if you had ultimate control over what happened to you (which, if you haven't noticed yet, you don't), you would probably miss out on opportunities for growth, change, and unexpected forks in the road taking you where you never imagined you'd be.

That said, it's still good to have goals. Goals give you a direction to work toward. You won't become a strong leader without a focus on communicating well, cultivating empathy, knowing your job and your employees' jobs, learning constantly, using tools, and more. Being a leader means knowing yourself, understanding your past, and setting goals for the future.

Consequences of Not Setting Goals

If you don't know what your goals are, you'll go down unproductive paths leading to stress because your life has no sense of purpose. This can create friction in personal and professional relationships because you're agreeing to or doing something contrary to what you really want. Sailing in a boat without a rudder will get you somewhere, but it's unlikely you'll end up where you want to be!

Bottom line: don't let anyone navigate the path for you. Setting a course based on the shifting winds of other people's opinions about what you should do is a terrible plan. Contemplate your past, your present, your desires for the future, and the path you need to take to arrive at your perfect day… then set sail and go!

REMEMBER

Prioritize purposeful rest and align your work with your life's long-term 'why' to sustain motivation and achieve overall life fulfillment.

SWOT ANALYSIS SHEET

STRENGTHS	WEAKNESSES

OPPORTUNITIES	THREATS

CHAPTER 29

Are You Sure? Part Two

"If a man will begin with certainties, he shall end in doubts; but if he will be content to begin with doubts, he shall end in certainties."

— FRANCIS BACON, THE ADVANCEMENT OF LEARNING [49]

Seriously though—are you sure you want to be a leader? We all know it and you can say it: people suck, so why be a leader? Congratulations! You read part two correctly. It's hard enough to get from point A to point B in this line of work on your own… do you really want to put yourself in a position where people can influence how well you do your job? Leadership is guiding people today to become better people in the future. It's also finding out other people don't want to be better or do better… and then figuring out how much of each type of person (willing to improve or not) you want and need around you.

Drawbacks of Leadership

You'll get yelled at for trying to help. You will disappoint people. Some employees won't understand why they can't earn more money or get a promotion. Some will expect you to say yes to everything and give them the best of everything, and if you don't, it's your fault. You'll have more responsibilities without getting a fraction of what those extra responsibilities are worth.

…So Why Be a Leader?

I am a leader because I can't do everything. I need other people to do their parts, and if I can make their lives easier by providing tools and resources, I want to. Sometimes I can't, and they just have to shut up and color until I find an opportunity to make it better. I want people to have outstanding work environments where they feel appreciated. I want my employees to know they have someone on their side at work and in life. I'm not perfect—I suck sometimes—but I do this because I want others to be better than I am. It won't always work out, but at least I can say I tried.

Conclusion

"The end is never the end. It's always the beginning of something."

— KATE LORD BROWN, THE PERFUME GARDEN [50]

In this book, I've shared the concepts that have been helpful to me as I've grown into a leadership role as a government contractor. I've shared from personal life experience the most impactful moments (in the hope you won't make the same mistakes I did). Maybe the entire book won't apply to you. Even if it doesn't, I hope you can take something away from it to implement in your own life so you can successfully navigate the future.

Remember how, in the introduction, I said I was writing this book for myself as much as I was for you? I hope you can see by now that these principles and topics won't only benefit you, but the people around you. People will benefit from your strength, knowledge, and hard-earned skills. You'll make the lives of those around you easier just by your presence. Strive to make lives better, and your life will improve as well.

I'm not sure if this book will result in the outcome I want (for my readers and myself). I hope it does—I hope it opens eyes. I would love to see people start to communicate positively. Maybe some people will get better at communicating, planning for the future, and building professional relationships. I'd love for this book to add to my accountability and drive to be responsive, empathetic, engaged, and a strong communicator. We are our own harshest critics, and if we hold ourselves to a higher standard, we'll naturally start aiming to make other people's lives better. Whether you choose to be a lifetime support contractor, want to grow into a leadership role with management responsibilities, or are just reading this book because someone gave it to you, I hope you'll be better for having read it.

You are the most important factor in your future. Make sure you can look in the mirror every morning and say, "I am improving." Take the time to learn who you are, what you want, and what path you should chase. Learn the skills to be successful, and know you'll need to devote yourself to continual learning. Do all you can to gain personal satisfaction and happiness, then do what you can to hold onto that happiness for the rest of your life (even if what makes you happy changes over time).

Things to Remember

Here are some key reminders for you:
- Overcommunicate correctly (Ch 4 - Learn the Craft)
- "You are so right, but you are so wrong" (Ch 4 - Learn the Craft)
- Vent the right way (Ch 5 - Deal with the System)
- Know why you're doing what you're doing (Ch 7 - Keep the Government Out of Trouble)
- Find a mentor who is willing to help you grow (Ch 17 - Paths of Leadership)
- "Embrace the suck" (Ch 17 - Paths of Leadership)
- "Kill stupid" (Ch 17 - Paths of Leadership)
- Take ownership (Ch 19 - How to Support Employees)
- As a leader, always provide the "why" (Ch 19 - How to Support Employees)
- Life is hard, work is hard, and balancing both is really hard, but if you navigate it well, you'll find success in both your professional and personal lives (Ch 28 - Take a Minute for Yourself)

Final Words

A post-conclusion conclusion? The world is always changing, right? Why wouldn't there be an addendum to the ending?

Here's my point: everything is constantly changing, evolving, and growing. Your future in government support might not go as you thought it would. You might not take the road you think you will. That's okay, because you can always change, evolve, and grow to be better. We can't control the world around us. We can't control what happens to us (in our professional lives or our personal lives). Control what you can and let the world handle the rest. Be the best "you" possible and focus on building a solid foundation and personal brand so if you're knocked down on the way, you'll have a network of people around you who can help.

Life comes at you quick—you never know who'll be the right person at the right time to get you to the next step of your journey.

Acronym Glossary

ACL	Anterior Cruciate Ligament
ADP	Automatic Data Processing
AI	Artificial Intelligence
ATF	Department of Alcohol, Tobacco, Firearms, and Explosives
AWR	Air Worthiness Release
CAC	Common Access Card
CEO	Chief Executive Officer
Common Access Card	Meaning
CPA	Certified Public Accountant
CPARS	Contractor Performance Assessment Rating System
CRM	Customer Relationship Management
DAU	Defense Acquisition University
DoD	Department of Defense
EQ	Emotional Intelligence
FAR	Federal Acquisition Regulations
FBI	Federal Bureau of Investigation
FUBAR	F***ed Up Beyond All Recognition
GAO	Government Accountability Office
GFEBS	General Fund Enterprise Business System
IT	Information Technology
LCAT	Labor Category in Government Training
MBA	Master of Business Administration
MDA	Missile Defense Agency
MILCON	Military Construction
MILPERS	Military Personnel
MIPR	Military Interdepartmental Purchase Requests
MS	Microsoft
MSR	Monthly Status Report
NASA	National Aeronautics and Space Administration
NFL	National Football League

O&M	Operation & Maintenance
OS	Operating System
OTB	Over Target Baseline
PALT	Procurement Administrative Leave Time
PCL	Posterior Cruciate Ligament
PDF	Portable Document Format
PEO	Program Executive Office
PM	Depending on the context, either Program Manager, Product Manager, or Project Manager
PWS	Performance Work Statement
Q&A	Question & Answer
R&D	Research & Development
RDECOM	Research, Development, and Engineering Command
RDT&E	Research, Development, Test & Evaluation
RFP	Request for Proposal
ROM	Rough Order of Magnitude
SAP	Systems, Applications, and Products
SOO	Statement of Objective
SOW	Statement of Work
SWOT	Strengths, Weaknesses, Opportunities, and Threats
TL;DR	Too Long; Didn't Read
U.S.C.	United States Code
VP	Vice President

Helpful Resources

Assessments

Employee Well-Being Survey

Assessment objectives: gain an understanding of the employee's stress level, workload, job satisfaction, work-life balance, and mental health. Understand the employees' current state, and identify areas where it would be helpful to intervene. Do this as a quarterly check-in.

Questions to ask:
1. On a scale of 1-10, how manageable is your current workload?
2. How comfortable do you feel discussing personal challenges with your manager?
3. What additional resources would help you feel more supported in your role?

Team Health Check

A monthly or quarterly assessment to evaluate morale and productivity. Obtain feedback on team dynamics, leadership support, and growth opportunities. It can be a quick email or a walk to the cube farm.

Questions to ask:
1. Do you feel your contributions are valued within the team?
2. Is there something that could improve your daily work environment?

One-on-one Check-In Template

A format to use during regular one-on-ones with employees. The check-in could focus on work-related issues as well as personal well-being. Works best as an informal, "drive-by" conversation.

Questions to ask:
1. How are you feeling about your current tasks?
2. Is there something we can do to help you achieve your goals or reduce stress?

Templates

One-on-One Meeting Template

A structured format for regular meetings with employees, focused on performance, well-being, and career growth.

Questions to ask:
1. What have been your top achievements this week/month?
2. What challenges are you facing right now?
3. What can I do to help you move forward?

Employee Check-In Email Template

A template for leaders to check in with employees, especially those who may be struggling or working remotely.

Subject: Checking in

Email body: Hi [Employee Name], I just wanted to check in and see how things are going. How are you feeling about your workload? Is there anything you need from me or the team to help you succeed?

Feedback Template

A simple guide for managers to provide constructive feedback in a positive and empathetic manner.

1. Here's what I noticed: [specific behavior].
2. This is why it matters: [impact on team or organization].

3. Let's talk about how to move forward: [suggestions/solutions].

Action Plan Criteria

Here's everything you'll need to include if you want to create specific action plans for your employees.

Onboarding Action Plan for New Employees

Create a guide including ways to support the employee for the first few weeks or months. Some examples: assign a mentor, schedule regular check-ins, or provide resources to help with the transition.

Action Plan for Addressing Burnout

Create a step-by-step guide on how to recognize signs of burnout, how to talk to employees about it, and what support options to offer (examples: more time off, reduced workload, professional counseling services, or any combination of the three).

In case you're wondering, here's what I do when people want to take on less responsibility, stress, or hours.

First, I try to find the why. What is the root cause? Are they just burned out (no balance in the amount of work and not enough personal gain from work)?Have they had life changes? (Marriage, divorce, kid born, parents aging...) Did they get put into a position that isn't aligned to them? (Wrong customer, wrong assignments, not technically skilled enough, not emotionally intelligent enough, not the right communication style.)

Once I figure out the cause, I work with them on a plan. Do they have life issues I can schedule around? Do they need a new position in a new office? Do they need more training? More education?

Does the contract allow for flexible hours? Work location flexibility? Do I have a lower LCAT that could change what they work on? Or do I need to find a completely new contract with a new customer?

Are they open to less money? Corporate support? Transfer to Business development stuff? Or are they getting close to retirement and are just complaining?

Sometimes people just need to vent and hear about my past struggles to know what they're dealing with isn't something strange…and some people need a total reset with a new company, and they need to know that is okay too.

Career Development Action Plan

Create a template to help leaders assist employees in setting long-term career goals. Provide resources and opportunities for growth (some examples include training, shadowing, or stretching assignments).

Training Resources

Workshops/Webinars

Create bookmarks with links to online courses or in-person workshops covering topics like leadership development, mental health, first aid, time management, or conflict resolution.

Books

Recommend reading materials that dive deeper into employee support. Some great options might include:

- The Five Dysfunctions of a Team by Patrick Lencioni (for building stronger teams)
- Drive by Daniel Pink (on motivation)
- Radical Candor by Kim Scott (on giving feedback with empathy)
- Leadership Land Mines by Marty Clark (shows how leaders think)

Online Courses

Platforms like Coursera, Udemy, and LinkedIn Learning have various courses on leadership, team building, and supporting mental health. Leaders can take courses on topics like emotional intelligence, conflict management, and resilience-building.

Internal Training

Encourage your company to build its own internal training programs or leadership cohorts, where managers can come together and discuss common challenges and share solutions.

DoD DAU Training

These are high-level job-specific trainings that can help keep employees up-to-date on current knowledge needed to do their day-to-day jobs.

Checking Employee Fit for a New Position

Fit Dealbreakers: Non-Negotiable Traits

Dealbreakers are qualities that typically cannot be changed or developed through training, so they make a candidate fundamentally unsuitable for certain roles. These traits are linked to the core aspects of how a person thinks, works, and interacts with others. Trying to force a fit can lead to frustration, burnout, or performance issues.

1. Introversion vs. Extroversion: A highly introverted person might struggle in a role that requires constant collaboration, public speaking, or high levels of social interaction (e.g., a sales position or team lead). Conversely, someone who is extremely extroverted may struggle in roles requiring deep focus and isolation, like policy research or technical writing.

2. Adaptability: Some roles require constant flexibility (for example, fielding and training events with constant travel), while others need strict processes and structure (roles in finance, contracts, or legal, for instance). An employee who thrives on routine and consistency may struggle in an environment requiring rapid shifts or out-of-the-box thinking (and vice versa).

3. Ethical or Moral Misalignment: If a person's core values or ethics don't align with the company's culture or the job's responsibilities, that can be a dealbreaker. For instance, someone who highly values privacy and avoiding potential conflict may struggle in a position requiring honesty and openness with clients or teams.

4. Attention to Detail: For roles requiring meticulous attention (such as accounting, data analysis, etc.), someone who consistently overlooks details or struggles with precision could face major challenges even if they get plenty of training. A person who pays great attention to details, on the other hand, could prove the wrong fit for a role where it's critical to focus on the big picture.

5. Rule Following/Compliance: Some positions, like those in contracting, finance, or legal support, require adherence to regulations, processes, and compliance standards. If someone has a strong aversion to following rules or enjoys cutting corners, it's unlikely they'll thrive in that environment.

6. Emotional Stability and Professionalism: Employees who have difficulty regulating their emotions or show unprofessional behavior (such as constant anger, impulsiveness, or dramatic mood swings) can disrupt team dynamics or relationships with clients, making it hard for both the employee and the team to succeed.

7. Cognitive Capacity for the Role: Some jobs require specific cognitive abilities, such as high-level problem-solving or complex technical understanding (software development and engineering are two examples of roles that require this). For those who are unable to handle the intellectual demands of the role, no amount of training will bridge that gap effectively.

Non-Essential Traits: Adaptable and Trainable

Trainable traits are not inherently dealbreakers and can often be developed with time, training, or coaching. If the employee has a strong foundation of the essentials (the core traits needed for a role), these traits are often malleable.

1. Communication: While effective communication is critical in nearly every role, it's a skill that can be improved with training and practice. Introverted or shy people might struggle to communicate in the early days, but with mentorship, communication workshops, or public speaking training, they can improve their communication.

2. Emotional Intelligence (EQ): Employees can learn how to manage their emotions, build relationships, and develop empathy through training, coaching, and experience. Someone who starts with a lower EQ can improve it over time.

3. Time Management: While some people are naturally better at managing their time, this is a skill that can also be improved with training. Offering time management workshops or tools (teaching task prioritization, encouraging them to download productivity apps, etc.) can go a long way in helping someone with organizational challenges.

4. Leadership Skills: Leadership is often developed through experience. A person might not start as a strong leader, but with mentorship, experience, and training, they can improve in areas such as decision-making, conflict resolution, and motivating teams.

5. Technical Skills: Proficiency with certain software, coding languages, or analytical tools is often teachable. If a candidate has the aptitude for learning new tools and skills, you can train them to be effective in that area. For example, someone who isn't familiar with a certain financial system or data analysis platform can usually learn it with training, assuming the government is open to the idea the employee can learn it on the job.

6. Cultural Fit (and Adapting to Company Culture): While a certain level of cultural alignment is essential for general comfort, someone can often adjust their approach to better fit the company culture over time. For example, a person who's more accustomed to hierarchical structures can learn to thrive in a flat organization with mentorship and exposure to the new environment.

7. Work Ethic and Motivation: A person's motivation or work ethic can be nurtured. For example, if an employee is not initially self-motivated, they can be inspired and coached over time to take ownership of their tasks. Providing goals, incentives, and feedback can help instill a stronger work ethic.

8. Creativity and Problem-Solving: These skills can often be cultivated through experience and exposure to diverse challenges. For example, someone who is more task-oriented but less innovative can be mentored to enhance their creativity through brainstorming sessions or exposure to new ways of thinking.

Support Bibliography/Notes

1. Widely attributed to General George S. Patton, Jr. online. At least two sources cite him as the author. Military Quotes. "General George Smith Patton Quotes." Modified August 16, 2023. https://www.military-quotes.com/Patton.htm. Patton Watch. "Quotes." Accessed June 16, 2025. https://patton-watch.com/pages/quotes.

2. Referenced by permission from Trinh Dang, 20th Century Studios: Office Space (Los Angeles, CA: 20th Century Fox, 1999).

3. Widely attributed to Confucius online, but likely adapted from The Analects into a modern vernacular. One of many translations of his works is listed. Ames, Roger T. The Analects of Confucius: A Philosophical Translation. Ballantine Books, 1999.

4. SRG. "What Can an Unqualified Hire Cost You?," Last modified May 5, 2021. https://srg4people.com/what-can-an-unqualified-hire-cost-you/.

5. Laurence, Peter J. Peter's Quotations: Ideas for Our Times. Morrow, 1977.

6. US Department of Defense. Office of the Under Secretary of Defense (Comptroller). Financial Management Regulation Volume 11A: "Reiumbursable Operations Policy." 7000.14-R, https://comptroller.defense.gov/Portals/45/documents/fmr/Volume_11a.pdf.

7. AcqNotes. "Financial Management: Research and Development Appropriation." Updated July 16, 2021. https://acqnotes.com/acqnote/careerfields/research-development-appropriation.

8. AcqNotes. "Acquisition Process: Initial Operational Test and Evaluation (IoT&E)." Updated July 8, 2021. https://acqnotes.com/acqnote/acquisitions/initial-operational-test-and-evaluation-iote.

9. AcqNotes. "Acquisition Process: Live-Fire Test and Evaluation (LFT&E)." Updated July 17, 2021. https://acqnotes.com/acqnote/acquisitions/live-fire-test-and-evaluation.

10. Zhan, Lexia, Dingrong Guo, Gang Chen, and Jiongjiong Lang. "Effects of Repetition Learning on Associative Recognition Over Time: Role of the Hippocampus and Prefrontal Cortex." Frontiers in Human Neuroscience 12, no. 277 (2018): 1-14. https://doi.org/10.3389/fnhum.2018.00277. Plater, Lindsay, Sandry Nyman, Samantha Joubran, and Naseem Al-Aidroos. "Repetition Enhances the Effects of Activated Long-Term Memory", Sage Publishing 76, no. 3 (2022): 621-631. https://doi.org/10.1177/17470218221095755.

11. Kobayashi, Keiichi. "Interactivity: A Potential Determinant of Learning by Preparing to Teach and Teaching."Frontiers in Psychology 9, no. 2755 (2019): 1-6. https://doi.org/10.3389/fpsyg.2018.02755.

12. Grosvenor, A., and L C Lack. "The Effect of Sleep Before or After Learning on Memory." Sleep 7, no. 2, (1984): 155-167. https://doi.org/10.1093/sleep/7.2.155.

13. Dresler, Martin, William R. Shirer, and Boris N. Conrad et al. "Mnemonic Training Reshapes Brain Networks to Support Superior Memory." Neuron 93 no. 5, (2017): 1227-1235. https://pmc.ncbi.nlm.nih.gov/articles/PMC5439266/.

14. Jäncke, Lutz. "Music, Memory and Emotion." Journal of Biology 7 no. 21, (2008): 1-5. https://doi.org/10.1186/jbiol82.

15. Kaur, Rupi. The Sun and Her Flowers. Andrews McMeel, 2017.

16. Chapters 8, 9, 20, and 22.

17. Angelou, Maya. Wouldn't Take Nothing for My Journey Now. Bantam, 1994.

18. While this phrase has been commonly attributed to T.S. Eliot, there is no definitive evidence it originated with him. Some feel it was a popular phrase before his time, and it could have originated from Montaigne, a 16th-century philosopher. The phrase is also the title of a book. Woolf, Leonard. The Journey Not the Arrival Matters: An Autobiography of the Years 1939 to 1969. Hogarth Press, 1969.

19. Andersen, Erika. "23 Quotes from Warren Buffett on Life and Generosity." Forbes, December 2, 2013. https://www.forbes.com/sites/erikaandersen/2013/12/02/23-quotes-from-warren-buffett-on-life-and-generosity/.

20. Judson, Jen. "US Army Faces Uphill Battle to Fix Aviation Mishap Crisis." Defense News, April 23, 2024. https://www.defensenews.com/training-sim/2024/04/23/us-army-faces-uphill-battle-to-fix-aviation-mishap-crisis/.

21. Bath, Alison. "Maintenance Failures on Army Equipment Stored at Kuwait Base Posed Deadly Risk, IG Says." Stars and Stripes, June 1, 2023. https://www.stripes.com/branches/army/2023-06-01/army-ukraine-howitzer-humvee-kuwait-10302759.html.

22. US General Services Administration. "PWS, SOO, SOW - Finding the Best Fit"." Last updated March 3, 2023. https://www.gsa.gov/events/pws-soo-sow-finding-the-best-fit?_gl=1*1tsq41i*_ga*MTA3ODYzMzU3OC4xNzQ3MzE5MzI4*_ga_HBYXWFP794*czE3NDczMTkzMjgkbzEkZZEkdDE3NDczMTkzNDUkajAkb-DAkaDA.

23. This interview is referenced online. Farber, Dan. "Tim Cook Maintains Steve Jobs' Beatles Business Model." CNET, June 12, 2013. https://www.cnet.com/tech/tech-industry/tim-cook-maintains-steve-jobs-beatles-business-model/.

24. Widely attributed to Albert Mehrabian online, but it doesn't seem he actually said these words. This quote seems to be a summary of the views he espoused in Silent Messages. Mehrabian, Albert. Silent Messages. Wadsworth Publishing, 1972.

25. Economy Act, 31 U.S.C. § 1535. Washington: Government Printing Office, 2020.

26. FAR Council. "Definitions," Code of Federal Regulations, Title 48, § 2.101, https://www.acquisition.gov/far/2.101.

27. Twain acknowledged this quote was partially borrowed from his friend Josh Billings (pen name: Henry Wheeler Shaw), a humorist whose works were published in several US newspapers. Footnotes contain information on Twain's book and an online resource stating the quote was originally adapted from Josh Billings.

    Bainton, George. The Art of Authorship: Literary Reminisces, Methods of Work, and Advice to Young Beginners. D. Appleton and Company, 1890. Quote Investigator. "Quote Origin: The Difference Between the Almost Right Word and the Right Word is Really a Large Matter—'Tis the Difference Between the Lightning Bug and the Lightning." Published September 2, 2019. https://quoteinvestigator.com/2019/09/02/lightning/#:~:text=The%20difference%20between%20the%20almost%20right%20word,a%20popular%20variant%20that%20appeared%20in%201890.

28. All Things Talent. "It's All About You: Building Your Personal Brand." Published April 9, 2019. https://allthingstalent.org/its-all-about-you-building-your-personal-brand/2019/04/09/.

29. There is no substantive proof Nelson Mandela said these exact words, but this quote is commonly believed to be a summary or paraphrase of the sentiments espoused by Mandela. Footnotes contain information about the commencement speech by Denzel.

    University of Pennsylvania. "Penn's 2011 Commencement Address by Denzel Washington." May 16, 2011, 7:18. https://www.youtube.com/watch?v=vpW2s-GlCtaE&ab_channel=UniversityofPennsylvania.

30. Clancy, Tom. Debt of Honor. Putnam, 1994.

    Examples include: DoD | 5105.4, "Department of Defense Federal Advisory Committee Management Program", DoD | 5015.02 "DoD Records Management Program", and AI-15 "OSD Records and Information Management Program".

31. Reagan Library. "Remarks at the Convocation Ceremonies at the University of South Carolina in Columbia. Published September 20, 1983. https://www.reaganlibrary.gov/archives/speech/remarks-convocation-ceremonies-university-south-carolina-columbia#:~:text=If%20I%20could%20leave%20you,-sticky%2C%20ill%2Dsmelling%20liquid.

32. Yes, I'm quoting myself. Why let everyone else have all the fun?

33. Attribution by Inc. Magazine and other online sources.
    Hammett, Gene. "Jack Welch Always Wanted His Team Members to Take Ownership of Their Work. Here's Why." Inc Magazine, August 10, 2018. https://www.inc.com/gene-hammett/3-lessons-from-jack-welch-on-leadership-that-you-dont-learn-in-business-school.html.

34. "Monthly" is used loosely—this is the government, so it can take a long time before issues are addressed. In this case, the monthly update came several months after the event took place.

35. Drucker, Peter F. Management: Tasks, Responsibilities, Practices. Harper & Row, 1974.

36. Deming, W. Edwards. Out of the Crisis. MIT Press, 2018.

37. Attributed to Firestone in several places online.
    Fairoaks IT. "Real Leadership is Power with People (Not Over Them)." Published November 13,2015. https://www.fairoaksit.com/2015/11/13/real-leadership-is-power-with-people-not-over-them/. Live Life Happy. "You Get the Best Out of Others." Published February 11, 2015. https://livelifehappy.com/life-quotes/you-get-the-best-out-of-others-when-you-give-the-best-of-yourself/.

38. Quote Investigator found, despite widespread debate over who said this, William H. Whyte was the true author of these words. (All relevant sources are linked in their article.)
    Quote Investigator. "Quote Origin: The Biggest Problem in Communication is the Illusion That It Has Taken Place." Published August 31, 2014. https://quoteinvestigator.com/2014/08/31/illusion/#221e2a49-5655-4c12-be52-daaf21094087.

39. Attributed to her by several online sources. There is no definitive proof she said it, but it is reflective of the sentiments she commonly espoused.
    Buckenmeir, ChesterIII. "A Great Leader Takes People Where They Don't Necessarily Want to Go but Ought To Be." U.S. Medicine, January 9, 2024. https://www.usmedicine.com/opinion/a-great-leader-takes-people-where-they-dont-necessarily-want-to-go-but-ought-to-be/.
    Biography. "Rosalynn Carter." Updated November 20, 2023. https://www.biography.com/history-culture/rosalynn-carter.

40. Bill Moyers. "A World of Ideas." Published November 17, 1988. https://billmoyers.com/content/peter-drucker/.

41. Villareal, Mark. Shortcuts Get You Lost! A Leadership Fable on the Dangers of the Blind Leading the Blind. Mr. V Consulting Services, 2016.

42. Churchill, Winston. "Give Us the Tools." BBC, London, England, February 9, 1941. Radio Broadcast. 36 min., 22 sec. https://www.nationalchurchillmuseum.org/give-us-the-tools.html.

43. Goodreads. "William Arthur Ward Quotes." Accessed June 16, 2025.https://www.goodreads.com/quotes/221493-before-you-speak-listen-before-you-write-think-before-you.

44. Frost, Robert. "A Servant to Servants," in Robert Frost: Collected Poems, Prose, & Plays, edited by Richard Poirier and Mark Richardson. Library of America, 1995, 123.

45. Several online sources have attributed this quote to J.C. Penney, but there appears to be no definitive proof he said this.
    Mourdoukoutas, Panos. "Ten Leadership Quotes from James Cash Penney." Forbes, February 28, 2013. https://www.forbes.com/sites/panosmourdoukoutas/2013/02/28/ten-leadership-quotes-from-james-cash-penney/. Saporito, Thomas J. "The CEO as Growth Leader." Chief Executive, May 8, 2014. https://chiefexecutive.net/the-ceo-as-growth-leader/.

46. Attributed to Robert C. Gallagher online by some online sources, but there is no definitive proof he said this. Other online sources say Earl Peace was known for saying this quote, but whether it began with him is difficult to determine. Sources are cited for each.
    Vanderbilt University. "Change is Inevitable—Except From Vending Machines." Published August 14, 2009. https://admissions.vanderbilt.edu/vandybloggers/2009/08/change-is-inevitable-except-from-vending-machines/. Holy Cross Magazine. "Tributes to Earl Peace Continue to Arrive from Alumni." Accessed June 16, 2025. https://magazine.holycross.edu/stories/tributes-earl-peace-continue-arrive-alumni.

47. This is an adaptation of the Tao Te Ching, which states, "The Tao is ever inactive, yet there is nothing it does not do."
    Lao Tzu. Taoist Texts: Ethical, Political, and Speculative (Tao Te Ching). Translated by Frederic Henry Balfour. Kessinger Publishing, 2010.

48. Francis Bacon, The Two Books of Francis Bacon: Of the Proficience and Advancement of Learning, Divine and Human, edited by Thomas Markby. J. W. Parker and Son, 1852.
49. Brown, Kate Lord. The Perfume Garden. Thomas Dunne Books/St. Martin's Press, 2015.
50. Johann Wolfgang von Goethe, "Knowing is not enough; we must apply. Willing is not enough; we must do," (often attributed to Faust).